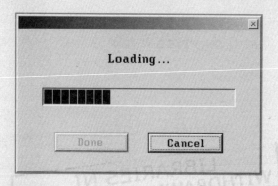

Escape

How a generation shaped, destroyed
and survived the internet

Marie Le Conte

BLINK
bringing you closer

First published in the UK by Blink Publishing
An imprint of Bonnier Books UK
4th Floor, Victoria House, Bloomsbury Square,
London, WC1B 4DA

Owned by Bonnier Books
Sveavägen 56, Stockholm, Sweden

Hardback – 978-1-788705-15-8
Ebook – 978-1-788705-16-5
Audio – 978-1-788705-17-2

A CIP catalogue of this book is available from the British Library.

Designed by Envy Design Ltd
All illustrations © Shutterstock
Printed and bound by Clays Ltd, Elcograf S.p.A

1 3 5 7 9 10 8 6 4 2

Copyright © Marie Le Conte, 2022

Blink Publishing is an imprint of Bonnier Books UK
www.bonnierbooks.co.uk

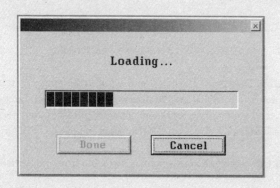

Contents

I

WHO AM I?

Brand New Start

Listen, I don't really want to be writing about the internet. I would even go so far as saying that the idea of writing about the internet makes me feel uneasy and that I would rather not be doing it. I'm not entirely sure why that is the case – I suspect it might be because it is such a part of me that I do not know where I end and where the internet begins. Disentangling the two will make me question who I really am, and does anyone really want to be digging this deep within themselves?

I was born in 1991, the same year as the World Wide Web. I took my first steps as the internet did; we grew up together, like siblings separated at birth but slowly becoming inseparable. I do not remember a world before the internet but I was not born in a world that had fused with the internet quite yet. Had I been ten years older, I could have discovered it as a novelty; had I been ten years younger, I could have just seen it as yet another part of life.

As it stands, my generation was the one that was able to see the internet as a peer, an imaginary friend that changed and evolved and grew as we did, and with whom we could go on wild adventures outside the real world. It was new and shiny and so were we; bright-eyed little humans, walking hand in hand with technology that was about to change everything.

It also changed us in the process; I have no idea who I would be today if I hadn't been handed a mouse and a pad at such a young age. I do not know what my personality would be, what sort of job I would be doing, what sort of friends I would have. I've tried to think about it before and I never know where to even start; I was born and bred online, and if you remove the life I have led on there, it leaves me with no life at all.

There has always been a screen nearby for me to glance at, and there never was a control group; no Marie Le Conte, shielded from technological advancements and – perhaps, perhaps not – different, more focused, less prone to oversharing to strangers. This is why I have always found it hard to write about the internet: it forces me into a self-introspection I feel I could do without. Still, something happened which made me realise that it probably is something I should look at more closely, both for my own sake and because there are some things which deserve to be said now, otherwise they will be forgotten.

The year 2020 was the year we lived online. It was the year work happened on Zoom and socialising happened on Zoom and dates happened on Zoom, and we were all at home but life, really, happened on our screens. For as long as I have been alive and conscious, the internet and real life have been getting closer and closer to one another, two separate worlds irredeemably attracted to each other, doomed to eventually collide. When they finally did, I hated it. I am the most gregarious person you will ever meet and the idea of sitting alone for days at a time fills my chest with lead; still, in those days, it is what I did. I did not work on Zoom, did not socialise on Zoom, did not go on dates on Zoom. Like a monk I stayed in my little rented flat, alone, obeying my self-imposed vow of silence. I had spent all these years with one foot in the physical world and another online and once they merged, I wanted out.

Zoom was only the tip of the iceberg, really; the most visible part of a shift that had been happening for years. I like to think of what happened as the life cycle of a formerly great bar: you stumble upon it by accident and realise it is wonderful, you tell your friends, who tell their friends, who tell their friends, the drink prices go up, it is rammed every night and suddenly you realise that what made it great was that almost no one knew about it. In trying to spread the joy, you let it slip from your hands.

Social media platforms are the same; Facebook was good when it was you and your friends and that one girl you met at a house party a few months ago, then your aunts and parents and colleagues wanted to befriend you and now it isn't the same anymore. Twitter was brilliant when you could post whatever went through your head and clusters of strangers formed around certain interests; it lost its shine when it became the plaything of trolls, fascists and bores.

What was once a great bar is now a sweaty, claustrophobic mess, where all the worst people alive are thriving and every potential future employer is a few clicks away from drunken pictures of you. It happened slowly but now everyone is here and it's too late to change that.

This epiphany hurt because I had always seen the internet as something that was mine, or at least something that belonged to the outcasts, the nerds and everyone else who had a good reason to want to escape from their actual lives. It has not been that space for a long time but it was easy to remain in denial, until it wasn't. On the bright side, this horrifying realisation was what brought me one step closer to writing this book. The era I was brought up in has ended; I am, for the first time in my life, of the old world. I am reluctant to try and decide when that era really started, but for the purpose of this endeavour, I have settled on 2005.

Two things happened to me in 2005. I was 13 and I had a best friend, Morgane, with whom I spent all my time, as teenage girls do. We went out together, coordinated our outfits and were rarely seen without one another. Towards the end of that year, Morgane had a go at me; like a jealous partner, she complained that I spent too much time on the internet, talked too much about what happened on the internet and had started having too many online friends. We had, until that point, been more or less the same person: two 13-year-old girls slowly merging their personalities into one. What came between us was that I had been attracted to the internet from a young age and she hadn't, and we were still living at a time when being online was a choice you decided to make. By 14, we were no longer talking.

In 2005, I also discovered a music blog dedicated to British and American indie music. As a French child, I had always been drawn to the culture of English-speaking countries, mostly thanks to Harry Potter books – another thing that unfolded as I did – and music felt like the next logical step.

Enthralled, I set myself the goal of learning about

every single band that blog had ever written about. I can't remember how many pages it had, but it ran in the dozens. What I do know is that you can draw a fairly straight line between the day I sat in front of the computer in my mother's living room reading that blog and the day I decided to write this book.

Well, 'straight' is a slight exaggeration – that blog took me to indie music, which took me to London, which took me on detours through London Fashion Week and living in anarchist squats, which took me to political journalism, which brought me here today. It's quite a long story, really, bits of which will appear later on. Still, my point is: in 2005, I was told off for spending too much of my life online, by someone my age who did not understand 'online', and I took it as an opportunity to embrace the internet even more.

In 2020, the whole world was forced to embrace the internet more than it ever had before and I shuddered and realised I did not want to be a part of that online world anymore. I did not want to be stuck in this hall of mirrors, where anything and everything you say can be distorted, taken out of context and held against you years later. I did not want to spend all my waking hours doom scrolling, seeing headline after headline after headline on how badly everything was going and how horrible so many people were. I did not want to share this much of myself on public platforms, knowing I shared them with malevolent forces, always ready to pounce and make my life miserable. That is not to say what follows will be all about me; I simply believe that my own experiences can provide a handy case study. This means I should probably introduce myself fully to you before getting started. It's only polite. So, to get it out of the way now: my name is Marie Le Conte, I am nearing 30, which means that by the time you read this I will be in my thirties, since the pace of publishing is what it is, and I am a bit weird.

I am not very weird, but weird enough that I was never very good at blending in with people. For as long as I can remember, I have been drawn to secret places where I can talk to other quite weird people and be my own quite weird self. I have, so far, led quite an interesting life but not a preposterous one, which is vital for this sort of writing. In the internet era, we all enjoy hearing from people who have done some things out of the ordinary, but who are not so exceptional that we cannot relate to them. You will probably be able to relate to me.

I am writing this book because I want to explain what it was like, being the first generation to grow up with the internet. I want to show the ways in which it built us as people, how the adults we turned out to be were moulded by the time we spent online. I also want it to reflect another fact that I know to be true, which is that we, in turn, moulded the internet. The web you live in now was built by us; if you look hard enough, you will find traces of us in all its corners.

If you want to understand it, you need to understand us, and if you want to understand us, you need to understand it. I can't promise you that I will cover every piece of ground that could possibly be covered; I don't believe anyone could do that. I can only write about what I know and the niches of the internet that made me who I am today.

I am not here to write about Big Tech, threats to democracy or who really owns your data; there are plenty of books for you to read if that is what you want. This is not one of them. Fundamentally, this is a book about people, how they build themselves, how they build and destroy each other and the tools we use to feel less alone.

We are humans and all we want, really, is to feel close to others, to feel understood and safe and special, whoever we are. What happened when we were given endless and endlessly malleable ways to find, talk and relate to one another? What did we build and who did it turn us into? From friendships and work to sex and language, the internet has fundamentally altered the world in which we live.

When I say 'us', I really do mean it; what follows isn't only my thoughts, but also those of the people who shaped my virtual upbringing. They are former sex workers, drug dealers or Members of Parliament and current journalists, influencers, academics and professional party girls. I wanted to know what it had been like for them; if their experiences mirrored mine and if their lives were changed for the better or the worse by being online pioneers. Not all of them will be quoted directly, but what follows certainly is a group effort.

Our generation was the first to enter this new reality and now the internet is no longer ours; there are new young people shaping the internet into their image and I am gladly passing it on to them.

I cannot pretend to fully understand what they do with it, but they do seem to have learned from our mistakes. The content they post is often transient and hidden; accounts are private and posts get deleted within days, if not hours. They are more polished, perhaps, or at least appear to be; they grew up knowing they would be watched and, rightly or wrongly, took it in their stride.

Many seem shameless in their pursuit of money and success, which I find uncomfortable and impressive in equal measures. Our internet was small and clunky; theirs is the place where a teenager can post a funny video and become rich overnight. Why would you not throw your hat in the ring?

They are also used to sharing the internet with everyone, which I never will be. Our internet was small and clunky but more importantly, it was ours. In those years, it was still odd to be spending so much time staring at a computer screen; real life was where people lived, we'd escaped to the margins by choice. Our structures and customs were never meant to withstand the weight of everyone else joining us and when they did, everything collapsed.

It happened slowly and was not obvious at first; only in hindsight did we realise that the internet we had known and loved was dead, a tragic victim of its own success. I would like to chronicle its slow and sometimes painful demise because I do not believe it has been done before, and everyone deserves a eulogy.

What happened when the real world decided to invade the internet? What did it do to our websites and to the way we talked to each other and met each other? What did it do to the people who came in and didn't really know what to expect? What did it do to us, the people who thought we had nowhere else to go?

I hope what follows can provide some answers, as well as some context for those who are still a bit bewildered by some of the internet's – and our – idiosyncrasies. I guess this is what I am trying to do here: provide a first- – and second- – hand testimony on what those crucial online years were like and what they taught us. So much writing about the internet in the 21st century is dark and pessimistic, but I'm not sure it always needs to be. We are going through odd and bleak times but so much joy has come out of the internet and so many lives were changed for the better. They are worth celebrating and – who knows? – perhaps there will be lessons to be learned from these occasional successes. Everything was in flux for a very long time, but the internet now feels more stuck in its ways than ever. It doesn't need to be that way: if enough of us want it to change, maybe we can make it happen.

Finally, I do hope this book will be picked up by people like me, fellow misfits who dreamt of a way to escape from their claustrophobic lives and accidentally built a new world in the process. It was fun and painful and weird and exhausting, but I'm so glad we made it.

Almost Famous

I think I can pinpoint the moment I realised my life would never be entirely my own. I must have been about eight years old, maybe nine, and I was in the kitchen with my grandmother. We were talking about the diary I had started writing every evening before bed.

'Where are you going to store your diaries when you're done with them?' she asked me. I had to admit that the thought hadn't occurred to me. She offered to keep them in a safe place for me as it was important to make sure they did not get lost. After all, I was going to grow up and become a famous writer and, after I died, people would want to publish my old diaries to find out more about who I was, who I had been.

She meant well but it was a terrible thing to say, really; it made me start living under the glare of an imagined future spotlight, which made me feel queasy. I have no idea if she was right; I have no idea if I will be a very famous writer by the time I die, but I suppose I'm on a path that could – perhaps, who knows? – end there eventually. Still, it does mean I became used to the online way of thinking before I even encountered it. If my diaries were to be read by strangers anyway, making the jump to sticking my thoughts into a blog felt natural. In fact, I don't really know what it means to write for yourself. Sometimes I feel overwhelmed by life and I pour my feelings into a Google Doc then never open it again, but even then, I make sure the prose is witty and insightful enough, just in case.

This is probably why I held my breath when I read the essay Tavi Gevinson wrote for *The Cut* * in 2019, 'Who would I be without Instagram? An investigation'.

Tavi was born in 1996 and started her first fashion blog at the age of 11. A year later, she was internet famous. In an amusing feature on young fashion bloggers from 2008, *USA Today* explained that 'Tavi's dad, Steve Gevinson, wasn't fully aware that she was blogging until she asked for permission to appear in an upcoming *New York Times* magazine story on the subject.' By 14, she had become a staple on the front row of New York Fashion Week and the sight of a lanky,

---

* https://www.thecut.com/2019/09/who-would-tavi-gevinson-be-without-instagram.html

quirky teen sitting alongside *Vogue*'s Anna Wintour was no longer absurd. At 15, she launched *Rookie*, a zine written by teenage girls for teenage girls.

In her essay, Tavi talks about the few weeks in which she operated three separate Instagram accounts: a public one, one for friends and close acquaintances, and a last one that was private and only for herself. On the latter, she posted pictures she deemed too braggy for the other two – snaps of her hanging out with famous people, memories of fancy dinner parties and a collection of daring selfies.

'It feels accurate to say that it was the only thing I made growing up that truly was just for me,' she writes, which is perhaps why the account only lasted a few weeks – if you grew up not knowing life without an audience, what happens when you're finally unobserved?

Well, it's complicated. As she puts it, the secret account 'existed just to scratch an itch, to satisfy the part of myself that had learned to register experience as only fully realized once primed for public consumption, but that was monitored by the other part of myself, the part that knew the actual sharing of these specific moments would appear inauthentic'. In short, something only ever feels real if it's been shared with others, but not everything can be shared.

A real person creates an online version of herself then the online version gets to decide who the real person is. It is not an entirely new phenomenon, as we will always tailor ourselves to an extent depending on who we are talking to, but the internet adds a whole other layer. Because we do not know who we are speaking to, we must tailor ourselves to be palatable to an invisible audience. Especially in those years before social media, there was no way of knowing who was reading your blog; as a result, the judging and calibrating had to be done internally. Instead of picking up on social cues or mirroring whoever we were in front of, we had to anticipate our readers' needs and tastes and project whatever version of ourselves we hoped would be the most popular.

The trick, of course, was that going too far and appearing too polished meant losing the very uniqueness and authenticity that people sought from personal blogs: the line to walk on was a thin one. In fact, the messier your life was, the more compelling your blog became. Tavi's example worked because the fashion world was still so formal in those years that wearing a mish-mash of high street and vintage looked novel.

A lot of the other blogs around at the time – at least the ones I followed – were run by messy young women with glamorous and complicated lives. They were sex bloggers chronicling their various one-night stands with questionable men; squatters sharing their tips on how to shoplift food and clothes; party girls talking openly about their heavy and frequent drug use. Laws were being broken, other people's boyfriends were being slept with, and it was all happening out in the open. Many of the blogs were anonymous but few of them were any good at maintaining their anonymity; there were first names and pictures and locations, and – even back then – that was all you needed.

It feels absurd to think about it now; how could these women have shared so much of themselves – things that could threaten their careers, their visas, their social standing – on platforms that were entirely open? Were they aware of how brazen they were being, and how much risk they were putting themselves through, and for nothing? After all, they were not influencers; there were no deals with brands to be had, no great fame and money to be found. They were just oversharing for the sake of oversharing. I wish I could scoff and judge but really, I can't; I was one of those young women, one of those idiots who could not stop themselves from blogging, no matter the cost.

It'd all started in the summer of 2005, when I discovered this indie music blog, the one I mentioned in the introduction. A few months later I launched my own, made online friends, decided that indie music was my life's passion, and that I had to go to Paris to attend more gigs. Being 13 at the time, I (not unreasonably) decided not to even attempt to broach the subject with my parents, who (not unreasonably) were clearly not going to let me travel 400km to the capital by myself.

Instead, I jumped on a train in mid-December to go see The Paddingtons, then repeated the experience in January and February 2006. That nothing bad happened to me when I was barely pubescent in a city I didn't know and drunk for most of my time there is quite incredible. That I decided to review each gig on my blog and expected it to somehow never make it back to any of my relatives, even more so. It did reach them eventually, because of course it did, and I was grounded for what felt like several decades – but that isn't really the surprising part.

What intrigues me looking back is that I clearly, tangibly, believed that I could have a public blog, which included my first name, age and hometown, and which was entirely separated from the life I lived in the real world. Like Fleabag, I could go about my day as seen by others, then turn to speak to the camera without anyone noticing. Well, other people online would, but they didn't really count; they lived inside the screen, like I did, and we just shared this separate world with one another. Though meeting some of those online friends in real life after enough MSN messaging felt appropriate, the opposite – offering real-life friends access to my online presence – never really felt like an option. As a result, it was very easy for me to write freely on my blog and elsewhere; words did not carry the weight they usually do when you say them out loud.

Thinking back, I suppose it also explains why I and others felt so ready to grossly overshare and write about every intimate detail of our lives. There is nothing stronger in a young person than the yearning to be seen, heard and understood; we were given the tools to do just that and overindulged. It is easy to think back and feel a sort of hangover from those days; passing shame from the amount of information we put out there. Still, it isn't entirely warranted – like trying to apply contemporary societal norms to, say, the 19th century, applying today's standards to our blogging days is useless. There are things I would have written back then that I would not write now, but back then, my father, grandmother, former bosses and current politicians were not part of my audience.

Because the internet and real life eventually ended up merging, we are now left without this digital twilight zone, a place where everything was simultaneously far more real than in the physical world yet not so real that we had to carry it around like baggage. In a way, it often felt like a playground; teenagers and young adults are made of wet clay and it is hard to predict what they will turn into. Being given access to this space where we could write ourselves into being was wonderful and I'm not sure I understand how else you are meant to figure yourself out.

Still, Tavi's words nag at the back of my mind. Who am I without an audience? Like her, I like to think that I'm able to be entirely myself online and as a result in real life, but am I fooling myself? Are we fooling ourselves? There are two more lines from her essay in *The Cut* that have been haunting me:

'I think I am a writer and an actor and an artist. But I haven't believed the purity of my own intentions ever since I became my own salesperson, too.'

Having had some sort of semi-successful online presence since I was in my early teens, I cannot differentiate between the person I am and the person I present to the online world. My thoughts often come to me in tweet format, and if they don't, I will naturally twist them into a shape that others could enjoy. Sometimes I want to share something wounding or banal that has happened to me but I know that I must phrase it in a way that is compelling otherwise no one will care, and why should they? We are online to keep each other entertained. If I cannot find a way to express a thought, opinion or experience in a way that I know others will enjoy, I will not express it. If I don't express it, it is likely to become something I brush off and forget about; if I have not typed something, it hasn't really happened.

I am very good at telling stories, in person and online, because I am terrified of people losing interest and no longer listening to my stories. If a blog had several boring posts in a row, people would stop visiting it altogether; if I tell one too many dull stories in the pub in a row, I worry no one will listen to me again. I spent a lot of time writing about myself because I believe oversharing is a way to try and fast-track intimacy; I was a weird child who was bullied and all I wanted was friends. By skipping the small talk and diving straight into things one should only ever tell people they are already close to, I thought I could trick strangers into becoming my close friends by default. Sure, it is the wrong way round – the secrets usually come after the friendship – but I didn't really have another choice.

Sometimes, even now, I will post something personal then realise I went too far the second I hit 'send'. It is a very physical sensation; it feels like I have prised my ribcage open and am showcasing my entrails to the world. When it happens I quietly delete whatever it is that I posted and I wait for the malaise to quietly go away. Still, I am a hypocrite; there is nothing I love more than people sharing too much of themselves. For as long as I can remember, I have had a deep, clawing hunger for people's secrets. I want to climb inside their skin and find out about everything they would rather keep to themselves.

One of the people I became obsessed with in those years is called Ingrid. Well, she isn't but she asked me to call her Ingrid in this chapter. She doesn't want her full name to be associated with her blogging years, even though her full name is not entirely her name, as she changed it some years ago to escape from her online past. What I remember from said past is that she used to work in a very trendy shop in east London, party every single night and surround herself with people who were as thin and beautiful as she was. Her life did not seem glamorous, at least not in the conventional sense, but it was compelling; she always looked knackered and her eye make-up was always smudged, like she'd applied it days or weeks earlier.

Her side hustle was to handprint T-shirts with slogans like 'USELESS FUCKING FEMALE' and 'COKE BUILT THIS BODY', which she would wear with little, else. Our paths crossed a few times once I moved to London and we eventually became friends on Facebook – because of a request I sent, of course. She left England in the early 2010s and mostly disappeared from the internet after that. Looking at her profile now, she is in her early thirties, has a young child and exercises frequently. I reached out to her and she was happy to talk; I was taken aback by what she had to say.

'Much of my writing was a cry for help,' she told me in an email. 'I was in a very bad place at the time. I had a lot of fun for sure, but there was also a lot of violent and destructive relationships, sexual and otherwise, pretty severe drug abuse, self-harm and lots of other stuff I wouldn't wish anyone to have to go through.'

When mephedrone, her drug of choice, became illegal in the UK, she decided the party had to come to an end: 'I was no longer having any fun and I think I started seeing my life for what it actually was – pretty depressing, that is! Almost overnight, I decided to do something entirely different. I went to university, changed social circles and all-nighters at squat parties were swapped out for all-nighters at the library. Seen from the outside, it was probably quite boring and, indeed, my readership numbers tanked. I wasn't too bothered though, I shut down the blog in my first year at uni to focus on my studies.'

This is when she decided to change her name, for reasons that were more practical than symbolic: 'I was featured in quite a few articles and interviews during those years that I didn't want potential future employers to see. One article in particular stated: "Meet Ingrid, the 20-year-old former drug dealer who's dreaming of becoming a diplomat". This was just after I'd decided to leave my old life behind to go to university. Three years later I was, indeed, working in diplomacy. I was very determined about the career goals I had and I didn't want any peers, colleagues or superiors to know that I'd previously been dealing drugs and lived that kind of life.'

What does she make of this life now and the fact that she wrote about it publicly at the time? 'You know, I wouldn't have them undone,' she told me. 'Every single day I think about how grateful I am for the life I'm living today and how different it could've been if I'd continued down the road I was on. Some of my old mates from those days are today very successful entrepreneurs and artists. Others are homeless or even dead. We are the lucky ones.'

Reading her responses worried me and warmed my heart at the same time; I had unknowingly feasted on the traumatic years of a quasi-stranger, but she had made it out in the end. I was sad her old blogs had been deleted from the internet and embarrassed by my sadness – how could I have the right to control someone else's complicated past? Then I thought of Candy.

Candy was this frenemy I had in around 2008, who ran a rival music blog to mine. I had my team, she had hers, we would interview the same bands and fight over who would get to go to the afterparties.

Candy was beautiful in the way that desperately sexual young women can be; she was very broken in a way that was glamorous when we were all under

25

the age of 20. One day I discovered her secret blog, in which she wrote about all her sexual encounters. I devoured it; could not get enough of it. She didn't know I knew about it and every day I would go back, hoping she would have posted about yet another man fucking her from behind while she was trying not to throw up from her comedown. One day I decided to link to it on my own blog and quietly added it to my sidebar; people discovered it, realised it was hers, and she closed it down. I have no idea why I did it; I knew it was a bad thing to do and I knew that it could only end with her deleting it, but I did it anyway. Perhaps, deep down, I wanted her to delete it; I'd stumbled upon it quite randomly but I could not un-find it, and it made me feel uncomfortable to see how much of herself she was putting out there. If I'm being entirely honest, I think I resented myself for being so enthralled by her secret writing; there is only so much rubbernecking we can do before becoming ashamed of ourselves.

I wonder if a similar dynamic was responsible for the rise and fall of what eventually became known as the 'first-personal industrial complex'. It is hard to know when it even started rising; I do remember it not existing, then existing, then being everywhere. It was probably in around 2008; everyone had their blogs and spilled far too much of themselves in them and suddenly, the media industry caught up with us. More and more publications were starting to understand that what works in print is not always what works online and they went searching for what people enjoyed reading on their screens. Personal stories written by young women was the answer. If you were around at the time, you probably remember the website *xoJane*, which became the figurehead of the 'oversharing for clicks' era.

If you weren't, here are some choice examples:

'The Story About How I Got Sober Once and For All, Which Yes, Includes Two Filthy Sex-Club Stories'
'It Happened To Me: My Gynaecologist Found a Ball of Cat Hair in My Vagina'
'My Former Friend's Death Was a Blessing'

xoJane's posts were especially jarring but hardly the exception; by around 2011, it felt like most of the internet had been taken over by women paid a pittance to write about something incredibly intimate, shocking or ideally both. New media outlets like *BuzzFeed*, *Jezebel* and *Salon* jumped on the opportunity to publish content that cost little – no reporting trips needed – but reliably brought in the clicks. Readers couldn't get enough of sordid personal stories and a generation of young women trying to get into journalism realised that a convenient (if harrowing) shortcut could be to write about their abortion, mental breakdown, rape or all of the above. Like everything else online, this trend faded over time; in 2017, Jia Tolentino wrote in the *New Yorker* that 'The personal essay boom is over'.

There are a number of reasons why this happened. The most obvious one is that people were tired and maybe a little bit ashamed of reading unknown writers mine the darkest corners of their lives for clicks. Another is that the media industry finally started to change its tune and enough journalists, especially female ones, called out publications for exploiting often vulnerable women because they didn't want to pay for proper journalism. The one I find more interesting is that it started to feel a little too uncomfortable. After all, the first-person industrial complex started at a time when people were freely sharing secrets about themselves on their blogs anyway. In that context, it wasn't that odd to see media organisations ride a wave that was already there. By 2017, however, the internet had changed; blogs no longer existed in the way they once did and we had collectively realised that if our families and future employers were now going to be online with us, we probably had to self-censor a bit more.

To give it a real-life comparison, the shift felt like

the difference between being on holiday alone and somehow ending up at a house party with random people and going to a house party hosted by your friends. In the former, it is surprisingly easy to get drunk and have unexpectedly meaningful conversations with people you will never see again, *because* you will never see them again. This is why there are so many memes about the strange beauty of chatting with random women in club bathrooms at 3am; sometimes there is a unique comfort to be found in strangers. In the latter, the circumstances are largely similar – small flat, drunk people, questionable cocktails – but deep down, you will always know that if you do or say something, it may come back to haunt you. You have worked hard to build an image of yourself and if you blurt out your darkest secrets to an acquaintance, they will probably come to see you differently, and share that new and unflattering image with others.

The confession also stops being stuck in a moment; if you post something on an anonymous blog or reveal a secret to a stranger, you remain in control of your own information. The blog can always be deleted, the readers don't know you in real life anyway, and the stranger will never see you again. Well, that was the white lie we told ourselves for a while; in theory, our blogs could very much be found by anyone – as happened to me with my covert trips to Paris – but that wasn't what it felt like. In any case, Tolentino was right to write what she did in 2017; by then, the era of oversharing was over. The way new generations connect with one another seems more shallow, private and transient; if they post anything publicly, it will probably be gone in a matter of weeks.

Then there is the fact that influencers – in many ways today's bloggers – have established a very different relationship between their real lives and their online lives. I hadn't really thought about it until Tea Hacic-Vlahovic, a blogger turned author, pointed it out to me in a voice note: 'In 2010 on Tumblr, we would go and actually live a life, and then come back to Tumblr and tell those stories; we'd share actual life stuff on Tumblr. Now, people are specifically living through Instagram, through social media; they're specifically doing things for social media, which is very different from what we were doing. We were having real-life experiences we later shared online. The approach to blogging was very different from the approach to social media.'

I remember those years well, because I hung on to her every word. A 'Sagittarius from Croatia', Tea is a few years older than me and one of the funniest, oddest people I have ever come across. She started her first Blogspot, *Crumpets*, at 21, while studying fashion in Milan. 'I just had opinions on the fashion industry; I was very disappointed in it and I didn't really know what to do with those feelings. My sister was like, "start a fucking blog!", so I did.'

Parallel to *Crumpets* was *Sugar Tits*, her Tumblr, in which she talked about the various nights out she was having and the various men she slept with on those nights out. Her writing was titillating but also witty and candid; eventually, *Sugar Tits* took off in a way *Crumpets* never had: 'My Tumblr was technically anonymous so it felt like a secret community, but you could still get followers and feel like a legend and a superstar, it felt really important.'

Tea's semi-fame nearly came to an end when she met Stefano, the man who became her boyfriend, then her husband. It was a whirlwind romance; I remember it well because it made me anxious she would disappear in a cloud of marital bliss, never to be seen online again. As it turns out, she shared those worries: 'I felt scared when I met Stefano and when we were deciding to get married. I was like, my whole personality is about being a slut. I was a sex columnist and a sex blogger. My personality, I thought, was heavily based on that.'

Luckily, both for Tea and her audience, little changed in the end: 'I think that sluttiness is an energy and a lifestyle. It actually has very little to do with how much sex you have. I think you can have slutty, rebellious, radical energy even as a virgin kid! Sluttiness for me was just one way to be rebellious.'

Though happily hitched, she remains more or less the same; the last time I looked at her Instagram, she was dancing in her room, semi-naked and in slow motion, to some absurd song I'd never heard before. Still, her writing is no longer as confessional as it used to be; instead, she has thrown herself into fiction and, at time of writing, is on the cusp of publishing her second novel. Tea remains online, but like everyone else mentioned here so far, the door into her private life which was once wide open is now only slightly ajar.

I suppose this makes us quite unique. By 'us', I mean the women around my age, somewhere between their mid-twenties and mid-thirties. We shared our whole lives with the internet and in return, the internet gave us the lives we wanted. I really do mean women, by the way; though I'm sure some men had blogs, this particular corner of the internet was overwhelmingly female. I like to think that our under-representation in popular culture had a part to play in this; if you will not give us characters and famous women who look and sound and live like us, we will simply find each other and fill that gap ourselves. That is an undeniable positive; though things seem to have changed for the teenage girls of today, we couldn't really rely on anyone to tell us what our peers actually wore, how they actually discovered sex and, in general, what they were actually up to. Ingrid arguably was not an ideal role model but I still felt closer to her than some *Cosmopolitan* article teaching me how to survive on crackers and water in order to fit into tight jeans.

Still, I do wonder how healthy it really was for us to collectively start adoring people purely for who they were. I just sat at my computer every evening and read about the mundane lives of random young women and I was obsessed with them. I also spent my evenings writing about my own mundane life and soon started meeting other random kids who were obsessed with me; the first time someone recognised me in public and gushed, I was 15. It was, and is, disconcerting precisely because none of us really were special and it is tough to explain what it feels like to be a little bit famous for no obvious reason.

It happens all the time now, from reality TV stars and influencers to whoever becomes flavour of the month on TikTok or wherever else, but it was a novel phenomenon at the time and we had no playbook for how to deal with it.

I asked Tea about it and she felt the same: 'When people stop me on the street, it's really bizarre because I'm still from the generation where, like, you're only famous if you're a pop star, or a bestselling author or TV host. So people stopping me to be like, "I know you from the internet", it just feels silly to me. I'm always overwhelmed with gratitude but I'm shocked by it.'

Then-prominent blogger Emily Gould explained this discomfort well in 2008, in an essay for *The New York Times*: 'I started seeing a therapist again, and we talked about my feelings of being inordinately scrutinized. "It's important to remember that you're not a celebrity," she told me. How could I tell her, without coming off as having delusions of grandeur, that, in a way, I was?'

As she explained later in the piece, she knew, of course, that she was not an A-list actress or someone most people would recognise as 'famous'. Still, people sometimes recognised her in the street and she had dedicated readers online; she wasn't famous but she wasn't quite no one either.

In this context, her point about scrutiny is a salient one: if we deem someone to be famous, we feel we gain the right to judge them, critique their behaviour and talk to them as if they weren't an entirely real person. Sometimes it is bleakly funny: I was once walking down Oxford Street hungover and needed the bathroom, so I walked into Topshop to use theirs. While queuing, I was approached by an overenthusiastic young man eager to talk to Marie from the internet. I didn't have the heart to tell him that it really was not a good time: instead, I did my best to be pleasant and engaging while desperately hoping for a stall to become free.

Sometimes it is crushing. It is easy for me to look back on my blogging days with rose-tinted glasses but, when I went through the comments people posted on my blog in 2007 or 2008, I was taken aback by the sheer brutality of them. Some of these teenagers hated me; they seemingly hated me more than anyone they had ever met before. They hated the bands I listened to, the books I read, the way I dressed, the way I looked. They hated me so much, they wanted to keep telling me they hated me. That is, I suppose, a somewhat darker truth about online semi-personalities; controversial figures will always fare better than bland ones, and if a lot of people really really like you, it is essentially guaranteed that a lot of people really really won't.

That I had forgotten about the viciousness of it all probably means that I did survive it easily, but it did make me think about this line in Tavi's essay again, 'I haven't believed the purity of my own intentions ever since I became my own salesperson'. It is one thing to have built yourself a personality based on how you hoped the internet would see you, but another to have been critiqued for every aspect of your personality by complete strangers from the beginning of your teenage years. What did I like but give up on because I was attacked for liking it? What did I defiantly decide to keep liking or even start loving to spite the people who attacked me for it?

You could argue that similar thought processes take place in each and every young person who gets bullied in real life, but I think this is deeper. Having been bullied online and offline, I can tell you that the latter was more superficial; I was bullied for being short for my age, for wearing eccentric clothes and for being a bit of a nerd. On the internet, I bared my soul and opened myself up to the world in the hope of receiving affection, kinship and understanding, and I was bullied for it. It physically hurt more when the boys in my year invented a game called 'Marie Rugby', in which I was the ball, but I doubt it really changed who I was on a fundamental level.

By comparison, online mean girls are probably the ones I should thank for my largely successful online life; by being told from a young age which aspects of my personality were the most objectionable, I was able to create a version of myself that was more palatable to more people. I was able to optimise myself further, to the extent that I do not know how else I could have turned out. The one problem with this, and the thing that terrifies me so much I can't bear to think about it for too long, is that I have no idea what and who I would become if I were to lose my semi-fame and constant impetus to self-optimise.

I wonder if the women I have mentioned here – Tavi, Tea, Emily, Jia – feel the same, since they are all, to different extents, still in the public eye. I do not know who I am if I do not have access to an audience that can validate me when I need it to, reassure me when I need it to and call me out on my self-indulgence when I need it to. It is hard to write because it makes me sound vain, but I have never known anything else. I have accrued very little wealth and only moderate career success from my online quasi-notoriety, but that doesn't matter. What does is that I only fell into my first ever relationship at the age of 29 and had never felt the need to be in one before that, and that I have perhaps been less reliant on the close friendships others often seek. I am close to my family but not that close; I am freelance because I do not feel the need to have colleagues I see every day.

I do not feel a need for any of those things because the internet plays all these roles in my life, and has done so for a very long time. I worry that written down, it seems tragic; to be truthful, I have no idea if it is. I lead a nice life. I do have friends and I do talk to my mother on the phone once a week. I do not feel unfulfilled; I have found a way of living that works for me. Still, I do wonder what will happen to me when I grow older and the internet changes beyond recognition. I wonder what will happen to all these women around my age who grew up the way that I did. I wonder what is happening to today's teenage girls, who are already savvy enough not to put their entire selves onto the internet and wait for the internet to embrace them. I will always write thinking that someone somewhere will one day be reading what I wrote; I have never fully belonged to myself and I never will. It took a village to raise me and without the village I am no one.

Never Meant to Hurt You

There are two interviews I did not include in the last chapter but would still like to mention. I didn't know how to fit in their quotes, which should have been relevant, because they made me quite sad and sometimes it can be tough to know what to do with things that make you a bit sad.

One was with Arabelle Sicardi, a beauty writer and former Tumblr blogger whose work and life I have followed for years. I came across them about a dozen years ago, because a selfie of theirs kept getting reposted on my dashboard. They had deep green hair and bright red eyeshadow and looked entirely androgynous, nearly alien-like.

I asked them why they had more or less disappeared

from the internet and no longer shared as much of themselves as they used to. I expected the response to mention growing up – they're in their late twenties – or perhaps losing their interest in blogging as it is no longer a done thing. 'Was becoming more guarded even a conscious choice?' I asked over on WhatsApp. 'Yes, years of stalking does that to a person,' they replied. 'Sad but true!'

This was particularly gutting because I had not even considered it as a possibility. I knew they were more high-profile than I ever was, but I had been too naive to realise that a certain level of online fame would come with such drawbacks. We were just kids! None of it was real! Well, not for everyone.

Following that exchange, I emailed another acquaintance I knew to be especially popular online. I hadn't seen them in a few years but some googling revealed that they had become surprisingly famous, which had entirely passed me by – I guess we all live in our own little internets after all. They were keen to talk but not to be named, which is perhaps understandable given what they had to say.

'I don't think there's any safe way for direct fan – artist friendships or relationships to exist, and I shut down anyone who tries,' they wrote. 'I wish it was possible to pick not just a stage name, but a stage face. I'm envious of people who can wear a mask or hide behind an avatar, but I also know that I get a lot of opportunities just because I'm not anonymous.

'I have to turn down events that I really want to go to, because I know there will be creeps there. The best outcome is that I'm an awkward distraction; the worst case is that I'm a security risk. Either way I'm going to have a bad time.'

They have had their fair share of stalkers as well and try not to meet any friends in public anymore. It is of course dreadful, but it feels worth pointing out how absurd it feels as well. In order to have this small and careful a life, a person in more traditional entertainment would have to be incredibly famous and presumably quite rich.

I don't believe my friend is, but because their work is based on the internet, people feel they deserve more of them than they would of another type of celebrity. Actors and singers can have obsessive fans, but they are in a small minority; everyone else makes do with scurrilous stories in gossip magazines. Becoming famous online often means acting like you are the personal friend of ten people; a hundred people; a thousand people; too many people to count.

Because a relationship built through a computer screen often feels more intimate than one built at gigs or in cinemas, it suddenly becomes easier for people to have unacceptable demands. If someone once acknowledged the comment you left them or brought you into their personal life in some way, how do you know where the line is? It may be obvious to the well-adjusted, but given the lack of established societal rules, it can be easier for well-meaning passion to tip into a darker territory.

I suppose it was always going to be the flipside of a culture in which we poured so much of ourselves into the internet. We did it because it felt like an easy way to create deep connections almost instantly. The trick, of course, was that we did not get to choose who we were making those connections with.

If you drop hundreds of messages in bottles across the ocean, some of them will eventually fall into the wrong hands. Perhaps our parents were right when they told us to be careful on the internet because we didn't know who else was on it. On balance, I'm glad we ignored them – but then I guess I would say that, as one of the lucky ones.

2

WHO ARE YOU?

Alone Together

There is a tweet from November 2019 that I think about a lot. It appeared, went viral, was mocked, then disappeared again in the space of about a week. It has remained lodged in a corner of my brain ever since. In it, @fyeahmfabello wrote: 'Someone reached out and asked for an example of how you can respond to someone if you don't have the space to support them. I offered this template.'

Below it was a screengrab of a message, which read: 'Hey! I'm so glad you reached out. I'm actually at capacity/helping someone else who's in crisis/dealing with some personal stuff right now, and I don't think I can hold appropriate space for you. Could we connect [later date or time] instead/Do you have someone else you could reach out to?'

ESCAPE

It became a meme and a joke because the phrasing was clunky and it sounded like it had been work-shopped by an HR department. As people on Twitter argued, this is not what friendship should be like; friendship should not involve message templates and verbs like 'reaching out'. I am not entirely sure I agree; though I would never make use of the message above, I largely saw it as a clumsy attempt to solve a problem no one is acknowledging.

To go even further, I would argue that the post is interesting not in and of itself, but because of what it represents. Within it are contained many of the ways in which the internet has changed the way our friendships function. It is awkward because it is trying to address issues that are so new we are not sure how to approach them.

I'll explain.

* * *

One of my most strongly held beliefs is that most children and teenagers are little sociopaths. I have no idea if the field of psychology would back me up on this and I have no interest in finding out. If they do not agree with me, they must be wrong – I was young once, I remember it well.

The specific incident I have in mind took place at

some point in 2004. I was 12 and studying at a private Catholic school and everyone hated me. Well, not quite everyone; I had managed to befriend two other girls, Coralie and Marina, because everyone hated them as well. Ours was a union of convenience: we had little in common, but no one else would come anywhere near us, so we became friends by default.

Like a temporarily embarrassed millionaire, I was convinced that they were mere placeholders, only my friends because the school offered few other options. Coralie especially was not someone I wanted to keep in my life for long, as her overly earnest dorkiness put me off. I explained this to Marina one evening on MSN Messenger, in a very matter-of-fact way. The one issue, it quickly turned out, was that I'd opened the wrong window and had instead told Coralie exactly what I made of her.

It was mortifying but we remained friends in the end, because I suspect that deep down, she knew that everything I'd said had been true. Still, I remember the jolt of panic I felt when I realised my mistake. It was over 15 years ago and I can still feel the urge to throw my monitor out the window, hoping it would somehow help. The other reason I remember this incident is because it marked the end of an era.

Until the autumn of 2005, I used MSN Messenger to talk to people I already knew, from school or my circus classes. Those conversations merely complemented the ones we had in person. Because it was not possible to meet people on MSN, the platform existed only as another space in which pre-existing relationships could blossom.

We can call this the second stage of the internet. The first involved losing yourself online and doing so alone; the second was coming home from school and logging on to talk to the people you had just spent your whole day with. It was life-enhancing but not quite life-changing yet; for those of us who struggled with the act of making friends, giving us other ways in which to talk to those (largely non-existent) friends was a bit pointless. The third stage, when we became able to meet people online and build our friendships there, was the real turning point.

I spoke to my friend Io Dodds about it, because she is a tech reporter and someone who is neurodivergent like me, but also because she is one of the cleverest people I know. She sent me a long voice note about what it was like to grow up autistic and awkward and not very good at making friends in real life. She has now found her people but it wasn't a straightforward process; had it not been for the internet, she doesn't think she would be where she is today. This is how she put it: 'On the internet, firstly, identity is plastic and fungible. That was very exciting to me, that you could be anybody and then tomorrow be someone else. You could adjust your identity on the fly, you could completely make things up, you could be pretending to be the person you wanted to be. The example that typifies this in my mind is the *New Yorker* cartoon that I think was around this time, which was like, "on the internet, nobody knows you're a dog".'

[...]

'There are also fewer variables to consider online, it's more under your control. You're not sitting there trying to talk to somebody and trying to figure out how to navigate things like...Who am I coming off as in this situation? What am I saying? What does my voice sound like? Am I acting weird? And what is that person really saying? And what's behind what they're saying? There's just a lot to be dealing with.

'The internet is much, much more simple. There's text – and often that's it, right? Whatever is happening contextually, subjectively, emotionally, socially, it's happening in this one medium, and it's usually happening slightly slower. It's right there, you can go back and read the wording five minutes later. It was so much easier to learn the ropes of socialisation and speaking to people and not being weird.'

This resonated with me because I have now got better at being social and coming across as broadly normal and friendly, but it is something I had to actively work on. In a way, the internet acted as our collective training wheels, both by making the act of meeting new people simpler and less overwhelming, and by putting less pressure on us.

As I see it, it offered us the opportunity to screw up then disappear. Social interactions as an awkward teen were tough because the stakes felt unbelievably high. If you managed to come off as weird or intense to someone at school, you would be reminded of your failure every single day, every single time you saw them. Plucking someone from the online ether to try and befriend them involved much lower stakes, as it was incredibly easy to pretend it never happened if it didn't work out.

Another game changer was the very nature of the friendships we started creating online. As mentioned earlier, the pool of potential people we could meet and like suddenly became huge. Once physical and geographical barriers were lifted, we became able to befriend people of any age, gender, sexuality or ethnicity, who lived anywhere in the world. As Io pointed out, this fundamentally reshaped the way we thought about our potential social networks: 'One of the things I felt [at the time] was that this must be some really revolutionary shift in social organisation, where people can be brought together for all kinds of reasons, and in ways that are less dependent on accidents of birth and accidents of circumstance and all that stuff that normally is dominant in whether people are socialising with each other and helping each other out, forming social bonds with each other.

'It seemed revolutionary to me that there was this technology and you could create communities that didn't work that way. You could sort people more efficiently, by what they cared about, by their passions, by the actual substance of their beliefs and their interests; the content of the character, if you will.'

This new social system was appealing because, among other things, it allowed people to escape from the rigid structures of youth. Befriending one solitary goth did not mean you were to become a goth yourself; talking to some weird boys late at night did not mark you as the sort of girl who would talk to weird boys late at night. It also meant that, as Io pointed out, you did not have to be all of yourself all of the time.

Few teenagers have a handle on their own personality. Being able to press different buttons by interacting with different, anonymous people online felt like playing a game of Choose Your Own Adventure, with the constant option of turning back and trying again.

Because using your real name online was not the done thing at the time, it also felt a bit like being Batman, or maybe Hannah Montana; one person during the day, another one entirely after dark. In fact, it felt like being both Batman and Hannah Montana, as you could simply change usernames for each website or forum you joined and no one would connect the dots.

Instead of being one uncertain and half-formed person, we could split ourselves into different personas, depending on who we were talking to. Did you want to be soft and emotional or coarse and edgy? Cool and distant or needy and passionate? Into playful sexist jokes or talking seriously about socialist politics? Rap or rock'n'roll? How about all of them at the same time, but under different names in different corners of the internet? Because none of the niches of the internet were connected to one another, there were no expectations for people to be well-rounded or coherent. It was pretty great.

It also allowed us to discover new passions and, once we found something that made us click, throw ourselves into them with abandon. Mine was indie music; in the autumn of 2005 I started a blog, named after a Razorlight song, and suddenly I cared about nothing else. I discovered bands, downloaded their songs, listened to them, wrote about them, hopped from MySpace to MySpace to discover some new ones, downloaded their demos, discussed them with other people who had been doing the same.

The main blogging platform in France at the time was Skyblog, and the main way to make people aware of our blogs was to comment on other blogs. Once potential friendship was established in the comments, one party would post their email address; the other would then delete the comment from their blog immediately and the pair would meet up on MSN Messenger and take it from there.

The first online friend I saw in person was Chiara, a 20-year-old art student who was horrified when we met up and she realised I was 13. We went to a gig together in Paris and I told her I had nowhere to stay and had planned to take the 6am train, so we walked around aimlessly for seven hours. She waved goodbye as I went to the platform and we never saw each other again.

A year and a half later, a woman left a comment on a blog post I had written about a gig, in which she seethed with jealousy at the fact that I had jumped on stage to kiss the singer on the cheek. We started talking then went for coffee as she lived nearby; 15 years on, she remains one of my closest friends.

Many people ended up falling somewhere between Chiara and Salomé; there were people I met a few times, others I talked to on the phone for months then never met, some who I still see occasionally. Sometimes they pop up in unexpected places. A few years ago, I went for a drink with a journalist; somehow we got talking about the Horrors, a band I was obsessed with as a teenager. I was so obsessed with them, in fact, that I ended up getting banned from their official fan forum – The Horum – for what can only be described as creepy stalking of the band members. The admin who booted me off was, it turned out, the man sitting in front of me in the pub a decade later. He remembered the incident well, to my deep, clawing shame.

He was an exception; for the most part, the people who shared my online passions between 2005 and 2010 have since turned into background characters, rarely playing prominent roles but still vaguely around. Their continued existence in my life is a new phenomenon; before the internet, they would have sauntered out of my life eventually, never to be seen again. Instead, we have kept following each other on Facebook, then Instagram, then Twitter. We do not speak but quietly like each other's pictures and posts instead. At some point I started thinking of them as 'silent friends'; when so much of online culture is sharp and hurtful, they represent an aura of quiet benevolence. Is 'friendship' too strong a word? I don't believe so. If one of them gets a new job and I press 'like' on the announcement, it is because it has sincerely brought me joy. If they do the same, I like to think that they are also genuinely happy for me. Isn't that what friendship is?

Another thing I like about them is that they are, in a way, completely stuck in time. Because they are people

I met when my obsession was guitar music, they have become the human embodiment of that obsession; cheerful ghosts reminding me of past passions. Most of my friends today are especially interested in British politics, because I have been especially interested in British politics since about 2013. I'm sure I will move on eventually and these people will become yet another ring on a tree stump, hidden away but integral to my structure.

But I digress. The point I was trying to make is that friendships do not end in the way that they used to anymore. The ones I mentioned are the ones I think about often, because they are very specific and very dear to me, but similar dynamics apply to everyone else, from former classmates to acquaintances you met twice then realised you had no interest in. If they got their foot in the door by befriending you on Facebook or following you on Instagram, they will remain in your life until you actively decide that you do not want them there.

What used to be a passive act – going for drinks with someone less and less often, barely replying to their texts – must now be done on purpose. Accounts must be muted, unfollowed, or unfriended, which often feels drastic if nothing bad has happened. It is easy to remain sort-of-friends with people because there is no entropy anymore; friendships are artificially maintained by social networks and cannot be left alone to disintegrate.

It is neither a good nor a bad thing. Sometimes friends lose touch for no good reason then regret it some years later, by which point it is too late; thanks to social media, it is less likely to happen. Sometimes one half of a pair feels that they have moved on with their life and would rather take their distance, not out of anger but because these things happen. Instead of slowly disappearing, they will have to make their intentions clear, or start rudely ignoring them. If they decide not to, out of laziness or cowardice, they will simply have to remain in that person's orbit.

Most of the time, it is a neutral change and people remain friends because they remain in the same group chats and end up going for drinks every three to five weeks, for no reason except that they may as well do so. What this means in practice is that it has become very easy to have more friends than you should have and for it to feel a bit suffocating at times. Well, perhaps 'friends' is too strong a word in this context; instead, it has become very easy, if you are online enough, to have too many people vaguely hovering around you and for it to feel a bit suffocating.

This was the first thing @fyeahmfabello's tweet made me think about; in an online environment where too many people know too many people, it is not surprising to occasionally panic and desperately try to back away. The feeling of being constantly surrounded can be overwhelming and the problem is novel enough that we do not have the tools to adequately deal with it.

Trying to cut someone off or become less close to them without unnecessarily hurting their feelings is a humble endeavour, but clearly harder than it seems. It shouldn't be a surprise; the internet was not built for break-ups, and neither were we.

* * *

One of my worst nightmares would be to be left alone in a room with nothing but a computer showing me every single message I meant to reply to then forgot. The number of inane, important, funny, touching messages from friends I never got round to replying to haunts me – I try not to think about it too much because it would keep me up at night.

I know I'm not alone in this; over the years, countless memes, tweets, pieces and variations on that theme have gone viral, proving that it is a problem many people struggle with. After 30 seconds of googling 'sorry I didn't reply', I stumbled upon Reductress's 'Sorry I Didn't Respond To Your Text! I Get Over-whelmed By Simple Tasks', @GeraldFordVEVO's 'hey man sorry i didn't respond to you for 3 weeks, i had to do a single simple task within the same 24 hour you texted me so i forgot' and many more. We are all online and we have all these friends and we are not very good at talking to them.

What I find interesting is that we rarely question why we are so bad at it; if there is a widespread behavioural problem, it is usually caused by structural failings. Instead of seeing their inability to respond to messages on time as a personal fault, perhaps people should stop to consider why it has become such an issue.

My theory – which may be wrong, who knows, but having one theory is better than having none – has to do with boundaries. Friendships, and indeed all human relationships, need boundaries to function. Before the internet and mobile phones, you could only see your friends at a time and place that had been arranged beforehand and was convenient for the both of you. You could also call them, I suppose, but a conversation could only happen if the two of you were at home and free to talk.

At the risk of stating the obvious, this meant that you could only speak to a friend when they also wanted to talk to you. You could ask for a last-minute drink to discuss something urgent but if they weren't around, there wasn't much you could do about it. The arrival of mobile phones marked the beginning of the end, but the mindset took longer to change. Similarly, the early days of the internet meant that you could email or message someone whenever you wanted, but could not reasonably expect an instant reply. Who doesn't remember 'AFK'? Who can now imagine being away from their keyboard for extended periods of time?

As often is the case with big life changes that did not happen in one fell swoop, I am unsure when we all started to feel a bit overwhelmed all the time. Perhaps it was at the moment we realised we could message anyone at any time while knowing that they could, technically, see our message the moment we sent it. We recalibrated our expectations and made our lives that much more stressful as a result.

Perhaps there is more to it, and it isn't just about the frequency of messages and the technology that allows us to send and receive them. Friendships had mental boundaries as well as physical ones; there weren't just rules about where and when you would meet someone, but also about what you could and would talk about with them.

Secrets were largely meant for close friends and so were hysterical rants; idle chatter was best with acquaintances, watercooler gossip with colleagues, graphic sex stories with wayward girlfriends, and so on. The internet changed this because it is much easier to go deeper with people when you cannot see them and they are not looking at you.

Teen Vogue published a very sweet and astute piece on this in 2014, in which they interviewed some teenage girls about their 'internet BFFs': 'Online friends seem to be more understanding. They see things objectively and give great advice and support,' 17-year-old Olivia told the mag. 'You can talk about things you may not be able to talk about with your friends in-person.'

'It's like you have an online diary that actually talks back,' 15-year-old Alyssa added, which I think gets to the crux of the matter. For a very long time, being online felt intimate and the people you met there felt just intangible enough that you could share your secrets with them without it feeling uncomfortably real. It was also easier to bare your soul to whoever would listen, if that is what you wanted to do; as Alyssa pointed out, it felt closer to talking to an imaginary friend than to another person. I wonder if there may also have been an unspoken rule, which was that we were all on the internet and not out in bars and cafés because we were quite lonely.

We collectively did not have the best social skills so we just threw ourselves into friendships with random people online because we didn't know what else to do. Many of us were quite broken, which is probably why I spent a decent chunk of my teenage and young adult years talking people I barely knew down from killing themselves. It became such a habit after a while that I did it without really thinking – I was sending heartfelt platitudes like I would write a message on a colleague's birthday card.

I have not had to talk anyone down from killing themselves in a few years now, but the principle remains broadly the same. Because we became so used to having intimate conversations online, it now feels entirely normal to get into heavy topics with friends over DMs or WhatsApp messages. It also feels natural to do so at any time of the day or night, because why shouldn't it? The boundaries were there because they were imposed on us; you could not turn up at your friend's workplace and expect them to suddenly care about your problems.

Once the barriers were lifted, we failed to put up our own – because we did not think about it or, on some level, because we were happy they weren't there when we were the ones in need of a chat. On top of this, we never really developed a language to deal with these new forms of friendship. When once we could say 'I'm sorry I can't meet you for a drink', there is now no real way to tell someone that we are not available without hurting their feelings.

There are no excuses because, well, we are always around; we may be at work or on a train, at our parents' house for dinner or in the midst of a breakdown ourselves but we could still technically talk. The only way to turn someone down is to admit that you do not want to be talking to them, or to ghost them altogether.

It is a bittersweet realisation; we were given countless new ways in which to connect with others and we were so hungry for them that we never stopped to consider that we could ever get too full. We also did not take into account that others would join us online eventually. It was relatively easy to keep track of your online friends online and your (few, far between) real-life friends in real life; when the latter started communicating like the former, all hell broke loose. Suddenly it was no longer enough to reply to messages about online matters from people you met on MySpace; at some point, your mother started forwarding you memes and those old acquaintances from work added you to a WhatsApp group about dinner plans. Suddenly there was nowhere to hide; all relationships were online relationships.

This is what brings us back to my beloved 'actually at capacity/helping someone else who's in crisis/ dealing with some personal stuff right now' message template. It was mocked by everyone, but, at the end of the day, it is no more than a gawky solution to a thorny problem. There are too many people in our lives and it is hard to get rid of them and they can message us whenever they want about whatever they want and there is no agreed way in which to politely let go of them or ignore their messages.

Maybe there is no way to solve this; the Lord giveth and taketh away, and so does the internet. It is possible that being occasionally overwhelmed and often bad at replying to messages on time is the price we must pay for our lives having changed for the better. I would have so few friends if I hadn't got so profoundly online at such a young age; even now, most of the people I know are people I first started talking to on Twitter.

My social skills have improved with time but I am still not sure how you are meant to meet people and make them like you in person; I never got used to doing it and it still feels daunting. It also feels a bit quaint and boring. As Io mentioned in passing earlier, it is surely better for people to get together based on their interests and likes and dislikes, as opposed to the place they work, the university they went to or the bar they frequent.

The idea of social spontaneity is charming but in practice it is often dull. Whenever I am made to spend any time with a group of people in their thirties who met as undergraduates, I thank the stars that no one on my course wanted to talk to me. I am who I am today because of the weird, interesting, good and bad people I was drawn to online; it seems absurd that geographical proximity or similar shift patterns should decide who you meet and thus who you become.

It is very possible that I just got lucky; in a different world, another Marie could have fallen down different rabbit holes, encountered different people and turned out meaner, sadder or altogether more alone. Still, looking down at the strata of my online life makes me proud of the agency I was gifted. As someone who was a bit odd and unpopular, I was thrown in with the Coralies and Marinas of this world, even though I deserved people who were more like me and they deserved people who were more like them.

It is easy to forget because it is so obvious, but that is what the internet gave us: the luxury of choice, which so few of us would have had otherwise. It is wonderful in its own right but also because friendships, especially those formed at a young age, get to shape who we are. No man is an island but it can be easy to feel like you are standing alone if you are a bit of a misfit.

When I was a child, I feared that I would remain just that, an island, forgotten in the high seas. At 13, on the night I went to Paris to meet with Chiara, I walked into the tiny gig venue and 'Where Is My Mind?' by The Pixies was playing and everyone was singing along. I cried in the dark for the rest of the song, because I had spent so long alone or surrounded by people who only tolerated me that I felt I had found my home. It was melodramatic, of course, but that is what it is like to be a teenager. Sometimes you are achingly earnest.

Is it bittersweet that this infinite pool of current, potential and not quite former friendships evolved to feel quite so oppressive? Of course, but I like to see it as a testament to how keen those like me were to find their people. We were the first to really build our lives online and all we wanted was friends; is it really a surprise that we didn't know where to stop?

No Place ...

It can be easy to feel quite negative about the current state of affairs, both about the internet in general and online friendships more specifically. They are overwhelming and now we are adults and things are less fun once you have grown up; that is a widely accepted fact. Because I didn't want to fall into an obvious pit of nostalgia and despair, I spoke to my friend Alice Beverton-Palmer, who I met on Twitter and who works at Twitter. She is 35 and her relentless positivity online often makes me think of her as a sort of real-life Leslie Knope from *Parks and Recreation*. (If you have not seen *Parks and Recreation*, try to picture a woman who is, among other things, relentlessly positive.) I asked her about the friends she has made online over the years, because I suspected that her story would be an interesting one. This is what she told me in an email:

'In 2013, I was in my late twenties and had a bit of a personal blossoming and really leaned into my pop culture interests. Those interests – Eurovision, drag queens, pop music, anything camp – were largely not shared by my mostly straight group of IRL friends, and there were gigs and club nights I really wanted to go to but had nobody to go with. So, I ended up using Twitter as an echo sounding for like-minded people. I just started tweeting about those things, and pretty rapidly started following people, followed who they followed, and discovered a whole network of Gay Twitter with the same tastes and vibe as me.

A year or so later I started going to gay clubs (like Push The Button at the Royal Vauxhall Tavern) and then meeting people in person, and years later many of those people are my closest friends. It's all a domino effect – follow Push The Button on Twitter, go to the club night, become a regular, become friends with the guys who run it, become a DJ there, become part of the RVT Future campaign to protect the RVT. It all goes back to an initial Twitter interaction.

I once tweeted about a dream I'd had about hosting a brunch screening of the Mariah Carey movie *Glitter*, and a couple of months later I was ACTUALLY DOING IT, because my friend Rob (the founder of Push The Button) saw the tweet, thought "why not?", and helped make it happen.'

(In the words of a once-quirky but now-irritating digital headline format: What Happened Next Will Blow Your Mind.)

'For a long time I treated it as a personal quirk that I was straight but had such an affinity with queer culture and society. I think actually being in queer spaces IRL was part of what made me reconsider my sexuality – I've since come out as bisexual – and I would never have been in those places if it wasn't for Twitter. Lone straight women don't tend to wander into gay bars (rightly so) but having friends who took me into those places, and how completely at home I felt, was part of what made me realise that what was being reflected back at me was a person who was actually queer.

Then once again, I realised that my existing friends (now mostly gay men) didn't have a lot to say about my new interests – whether Rachel

Weisz is hot (she is) or whether the sapphic sitcom *Feel Good* could have done with being a bit less depressing (it could). So I've started turning to the internet to find a new queer female community; I'm now again in those nascent stages of putting my thoughts online and seeing who responds.'

By the time you are reading this, I really hope that Alice will have found the queer women she is currently seeking. After all, there is nothing quite like the feeling of being among your people; it is joyous to think that the internet can still help with that.

... Like Home

I enjoyed Alice's testimony because it was quite straightforward. She developed interests; found that no one she knew shared them; went online; found some people who did. I enjoyed it even more because it provided an easy bridge between the topic of friendship and the topic of community.

Online as in life, it is often quite rare to befriend one person solely because you happen to enjoy their company. Most of the time, friendship occurs because of shared interests, beliefs or personalities. The difference between the internet and real life, however, is that the latter is, by its very nature, constrained.

You may meet a co-worker who likes the same band as you or a fellow student who loves comic books, but you only met because you worked or studied in the same place. Online, the possibilities became boundless; no matter what you loved, liked or even suspected you may be into, you could be certain that there were people out there who shared those interests. It was not always easy to find them, but still nowhere near as tough as crossing your fingers and hoping that you would one day encounter a kindred spirit. In a way it was freeing, of course; every eccentric will always dream of meeting people like them.

In another way, it was terrifying: were we really made to cope with this much choice? I guess it did not feel too suffocating at the start, because back then the internet was quite small and fragmented. It may have been comforting to realise that there were others, somewhere out there, who were goths or liked seventies garage or medieval history, but it was not always easy to find them.

Seeking them out involved a sense of purpose; once you had succeeded, it felt like hitting a goldmine. I don't know what it is like to grow up online today, when you are only a few clicks away from potentially finding your people, no matter how few, far between or odd they may be. I do not know what it means to realise that all these communities exist alongside each other and in semi-public view, and that you can choose to dip in and out of as many of them as you want.

ESCAPE

In the earlier days of the internet, joining an online niche meant committing, both because of the structure of those communities and because the people who were there at the time were obsessive by nature. Why else would you have spent so long seeking people like you? This fundamentally shifted our sense of identity, because identity is always malleable, especially so when you have no idea who you are.

It also sent us down a variety of rabbit holes, because there are few things a deep yearning to belong cannot overcome. Identity is not only about who we are, but also about who we talk to; had I been less drawn to the internet, I could have been someone who listened to guitar music but lived a relatively normal life.

Because I ended up in a sphere where strangers complimented me on the increasingly obscure bands I had heard of, I felt compelled to keep going down, down, down. I even went by a different name for several years; I thought it bland to go by my real name and started using 'Margaret Steinway' in 2007, after a song by a French band from the sixties no one remembers. Three years ago, I stumbled upon someone I knew in those years and had to fess up that it had never been my name; I had been so committed to the con that dozens of people sincerely believed my name was Margaret. Thinking about it now, I am nearly certain that I would still respond if someone shouted it at me in the street.

Of course it all feels a bit silly now, but things were different back then and you can only ever be a product of your own circumstances. This is what I would like to discuss here, I guess: how who we were decided who we befriended then who we befriended defined who we became. It is all about the limitless pool of people we can meet online and the fact that most of us both crave a sense of community and long to be unique. These desires can often be contradictory, but it is relatively easy to avoid that conflict in real life. Because your pool of friends is limited and everyone has a number of interests, it is unlikely that even one of your acquaintances will share every single one of your traits. It works because the dynamics are different; you are friends with these people because of life circumstances, but if you have a niche interest, it is likely to remain your thing and no one else's. That way, this yearning to both belong yet be different could be sated. Can it still be?

I talked about this with Alex Hern, who is the *Guardian*'s technology editor and someone I first met on Twitter some years ago. I mentioned his niche, nerdy interests and asked if he had got to them through the internet, or if he'd been driven online in pursuit of said interests. He rejected the premise entirely; instead, this was his take: 'The big thing the internet has done is made me realise I don't actually have any niche interests. It's sort of a mixed blessing: on the one hand, it's nice to know how many other people share my enthusiasm for this stuff, but on the other hand, it's a constant reminder of just how incredibly normie I am.

'At school, I thought I was an interesting snowflake, for playing mildly-artsy video games and having a standing order at a comic shop. Now I know that I am the most vanilla nerd imaginable. Occasionally, I wonder whether I should try and cultivate a really niche interest, but I honestly think, when comparing yourself to Literally Everyone Else In The World, the only stuff that looks niche anymore is going to be borderline impenetrable.'

Alex is now a well-adjusted thirty-something man, so can clearly cope with the fact that he is not in any way special. I have mostly made my peace with it too, despite clinging to the belief that I am the only political journalist out there who has tattooed herself and also does trapeze. If I'm not, I would sincerely love to meet others who currently fit those criteria. Still, that isn't quite the point I was trying to make – instead, I want to look at what happens when you realise you're not actually alone.

There are, broadly speaking, two roads you can go down as a teenager. You can either be popular or within reasonable reach of popularity, or you can be an outcast who gets bullied or ignored. If you are the former, you can derive joy from the knowledge that you have friends and are surrounded by people you feel you can connect with. If you are the latter, the only real way to feel good about yourself is to celebrate the ways in which you are different. It may look like intense narcissism from the outside, but perhaps that isn't such a bad thing when the only other option is self-loathing. Why see yourself as lonely and left behind when you can instead decide you're unique yet misunderstood?

Standing alone can sometimes feel reassuring, especially when there aren't any other options. What happens when, as Alex points out, you realise that there are actually thousands like you? At its most negative, it can feel like a lose-lose situation; not only are you not an amazing, one-of-a-kind snowflake, but the people who are similar to you only exist online and cannot make you popular in real life.

At its most positive, it can be life-changing: who cares about those popular kids anyway? You have found your tribe and you can live a fulfilling life with them; they understand you and can give you hope that you will not be alone forever. In practice, I suspect that most people fell somewhere between the two, though we'll come back to those who did not in a little while.

In the meantime, there is another point Alex made which feels worth exploring. In his email, he wrote: 'The internet didn't create any of my interests, but it absolutely reinforced them. In each case, I started off deciding to get into something – I vividly remember, for instance, being 18, and saying, "I'm a big nerd, I should read comic books", and just buying some comics – and then found good communities online that helped guide and develop my taste.

'What is also noticeable is the times I didn't do that, and how much more conventional I am as a result. For instance, I am heavily involved in a lot of board game community discussion and have strong views on the medium. I could never be arsed to join any beer community groups, even though it's something I'd say I have an interest in, and so my thoughts on beer are basically "I like nice beer :)" as a result.'

Similarly, my online life as an indie music fan pushed me to regard virtually any band signed to a major label as too big to bother engaging with, when my lifelong enjoyment of fashion still only translates as, well, liking nice clothes. Becoming a member of a community that shares your interests will often lead you to refine said interests, both because hobbies can often become competitive and because it feels good to have an edge.

If person A makes you discover band X, it is likely that you will want to retaliate by introducing them to band Y and perhaps even to artist Z just to make it clear that you have the upper hand. It is not an inherently negative dynamic; sharing your enthusiasm with others will always be more galvanising than discovering things entirely by yourself.

One issue, however, is that it can become worryingly easy to fall so far down the rabbit hole that you forget there is still an entire world out there. Human beings need balance and it cannot always be found if you surround yourself with people who are very similar to you, especially if you are young and not quite fully formed. We all yearn to belong and that is fine if it means learning more about bands or beer. What happens when the common trait you share with your chosen people is the very thing threatening to destroy you?

❋ ❋ ❋

Tumblr is the platform I have been on for the longest. I joined it in 2008, before Facebook and long before Twitter; sometimes I forget that it exists for weeks at a time but, for most of the past 13 years, I have looked at my dashboard every other day. I have three blogs on it: one to post pictures I like, one to post pictures I took and one that acts as my online CV. The latter set aside, I have never posted a single word to Tumblr; in fact, I have largely been a silent participant. I follow blogs and keep track of various bits of drama but no one knows I am there. Like an ornithologist, I hide far away and, with my binoculars, watch the birds interact with one another without disturbing them.

I remember the fights people had and the catastrophic fallings-out that unfurled publicly; I was there for the highs and I was there for the lows, and I remember them all. There is one subplot I come back to often because I think it's symptomatic of wider, systematic issues with internet culture.

In 2013, the *Atlantic* published a piece titled 'Social Media Is Redefining "Depression"', which argued that 'online communities like those on Tumblr are perpetuating ideas of "beautiful suffering", confusing what it means to be clinically depressed.' In it, the journalist quoted a sad 16-year-old, Laura, who argued that 'it's important for suffering people to have these communities online so that they can talk; it helps people who feel isolated'. Still, the article's main worry was that forlorn teenagers were too easily thinking of themselves as clinically depressed and, aided by the content they saw online, ended up self-harming or even contemplating suicide.

According to the expert interviewed in the piece, 'the solution lies in recreating the distinction between normal emotional states and the clinical condition of depression and the way to go about this is through education'. The way the issue was framed is interesting; it was not about mentally ill young people going to hide in ever smaller and darker online spaces, but about normal teenage angst getting unhelpfully pathologised. Though it did identify something that really was happening, it focused on the tip and not the iceberg. This changed a few years later, when reporting on the communities of Tumblr became trendy again. In 2016, a *Guardian* journalist wrote that 'Tumblr's mental health communities seem to be filling in the gaps for healthcare in the US, by providing support, information – and actual help from clinicians'.

The article focused on Mea Pearson, who was diagnosed with Borderline Personality Disorder then went on to launch a blog called *shitborderlinesdo*, and Gwendoline Smith, a clinical psychologist who started answering people's questions about mental health on her own blog. 'This, perhaps, is the most beneficial part of these communities, which cannot guarantee professional help or alleviate the burdens of people with limited resources to gain care,' the piece concluded. 'What it can provide is a community for people experiencing illness that is still subject to intense stigma.'

In a nutshell, seeking professional help for one's mental illness is daunting and Kafkaesque in most countries, and while talking to people facing the same struggles will not magically cure you, it can make your life a little bit easier. Or, as Pearson put it: 'It's knowing "hey, there's thousands of people who follow my blog who are experiencing this exact thing. Even if I know exactly what's happening, I can't stop it, I just feel less alone because of the online community.'

Finally, another piece published a few months later by *The Ringer* seemed to get closer to the heart of the matter. '[19-year-old Gillian Andrews] felt unable to talk about her self-harm, depression, and anxiety with her family and didn't have many friends when she began using Tumblr at 14,' it read. 'But here, she quickly realized, her mental illness was not merely accepted—it was encouraged.' Though the piece acknowledged that troubled teens would try to help each other and cheer each other up, 'the difficulty [came] not from these more positive posts, but in communities that might become too enveloped in a shared sadness'.

In this context, mental illnesses can easily be compared to Alex's board games or my indie music. They are very different in every other way but, when it comes to online behaviour, they can easily lead to the same logical endpoint. It is possible to simply like something in real life, but getting involved in relevant communities online will often lead to you seeing those passions as your entire identity. If having depression is the thing that finally gave you understanding friends and a comfortable online home, would you really want to let go of it, even if it is hurting you? How would you treat people who are trying to get better, if you know that they may well leave you if and when they do?

I talked about this with Julia Blunck, a 29-year-old Brazilian writer I met on Twitter and with whom I share a bond that only people who grew up on Tumblr can have. I wanted to have her take on this because I have never really struggled with mental illness and, though I saw those spaces flourish, decay then flourish again in real time, I was never really a part of them. I was a bit sullen sometimes, as teenagers often are, but never felt the need to seek the solace of those online communities. She did, and this is what her experience looked like:

'I didn't know how to recognise mental illness. My mother, a psychologist, would say things like "this isn't normal" or "you are unhealthy" but I don't think it reached me because when your parents say "you are depressed", it comes across in similar ways to "you don't clean your room" or "you have bad grades". It's an accusation, it's pointing out a failing. It was only with the internet, when I met other people struggling and I thought, "oh, this is real, this is an illness".

'A lot of people learned they had depression through their online experiences. That's extremely positive for that first step, but not so much when it gets to the point of "how do I address it?". Some of the advice is genuinely very damaging. "If you wanna stay in your room all day sleeping, if you wanna isolate yourself, if you wanna not work, you are valid" is just enabling depression. Don't do that. The conversation about how the people suggesting exercise and meditation are trying to hurt you is probably one of the worst things for mental health. No, these things by themselves won't solve your mental illness but they are genuinely very helpful, especially if you are, as many people are, unable to get professional help. Ultimately, yes, you should try to go outside once a day, you should try to be in contact with nature, you should try to exercise and eat better. To frame your upsetness with this advice as political activism for mental illness awareness is creating an impression that depression and anxiety are things that should be upheld and not fought. You have this bunch of kids creating a community that isn't about how you deal with mental illness, but instead encouraging each other to keep at it.'

'Any input that isn't just this relentlessly gloomy view of mental illness is seen as an attack on the group and gets you excluded. I've seen someone share their actual advice from a psychologist and be attacked for being "ableist scum". So you've created an environment where

people know enough about a given issue to create
an identity around it, but not enough to organise
properly and are actually making the issue worse.'

It is heartbreaking because it all started for a good
reason: sick and tired of being told to 'go for a walk; try
some yoga!', depressed young people turned to others
like them so they wouldn't feel so misunderstood. They
tried to help each other but enabled each other instead
and moved further and further away from a mindset
that could actually make them better. I am happy for
Julia because she eventually left those communities
and can now discuss them in hindsight, but I fear for
the ones who did not.

I also worry that they are not the only ones who
found themselves getting stuck inside increasingly
claustrophobic spaces. This dynamic can be witnessed
more or less everywhere on the internet, and is
especially relevant in what we've come to call online
radicalisation – but I'd rather come back to that later.
Instead, I would like to go back to the basics for now
and to the fact that on the internet, nobody knows
you're a dog. What I mean by that is that we were, for
a very long time, almost entirely anonymous online;
people frequently went by a name that was not their
own and a picture that was not theirs.

I remember joining Twitter in 2011 and calling

myself 'Young Vulgarian' and having some artsy, blurry picture as my avatar. Eventually I changed the name to 'Marie', the picture to a selfie and the name to 'Marie Le Conte'. Still, there are a number of people I talk to every other day on Twitter who remain anonymous.

What follows is going to look like an exercise in stating the blindingly obvious, but I worry it has become the (factual, benign) elephant in the room. If the people you talk to online do not know what you look or sound like, you will have to tell them. In real life, there is usually no need to constantly bring up, say, your gender, race or geographical background as they are all immediately obvious to anyone who is talking to you. Just like you would not start a fight with someone considerably taller and angrier-looking than you, life involves subtly calibrating everything you say depending on who you are saying it to.

It also involves assuming that people are taking these characteristics of yours into account when they interact with you. This is something I am acutely conscious of in real life because I am half-Arab but do not even look vaguely Mediterranean. Sometimes I will want to ask people in a shop if they are Moroccan because I think I can recognise the accent, but I am aware that a woman who looks like me asking that to someone who looks like them will not necessarily be a pleasant interaction.

I have tried to open with 'and I am Moroccan myself!' before but it only makes it more awkward; there is just no way around the fact that I am, as my mother occasionally quips, an Arab in disguise. This is more or less what has to happen on the internet; if, say, some anonymous account were to ask me where I'd bought a bikini I wore in an Instagram picture, I would only feel comfortable answering if I knew they were a woman – the identity of the people we talk to matters.

Well, for a long time I'm not sure we realised it did matter; for a long time, the complete anonymity was the point, wasn't it? We were faceless and we were equal; only what we typed to each other mattered. Our identity could be based on our sense of humour, our wry comebacks, our endless knowledge of a topic, or whatever else we wanted it to be based on. Freed from the shackles of our flesh and bones, we created a bona fide meritocratic society – or so we thought.

Because I did not spend a lot of time on the forums of the early internet, where this line of thinking seemingly thrived, I decided to talk to a friend who did. Hussein Kesvani is broadly my age and has had a career broadly similar to mine. We were both very online from a young age, became journalists, joined *BuzzFeed* because it felt like the done thing for very online young journalists, were very unhappy there, left, and now write about a variety of things, mostly online.

Hussein spent a lot of his formative years on *TOTSE* (*Temple of the Screaming Electron*), a forum that, *Wikipedia* tells me, discussed a 'wide variety of topics including but not limited to religion, sex, politics, poetry, drugs, illegal activities, [...] technology, music, metaphysics, sub-culture activities, the environment, food, and do it yourself projects'.

'I think "identity" has always been important online, in the sense that the early conceptions of the internet was a collective consciousness,' he told me. 'I've been looking at 90s libertarian philosophy around the internet and it's remarkable how much they cite Deleuze and Guattari, whose whole idea was that material systems produced by capitalism oppress individuals from their true state as "desiring machines", and that "cyberspace" would allow a relocation of identity in which without a body (i.e. the mechanism for capitalism to function) that "true" state would be more apparent.'

(I have never read Deleuze and Guattari and the very idea of doing so gives me hives so I'm afraid we will have to take Hussein at his word.)

'I was on a bunch of forums, but especially *TOTSE*, which was kind of like a forum for vice, nefariousness, etc. It almost felt like a superpower – by day, I was this young teenager without a lot of friends, very insular, not particularly a standout in any way. But in the evenings, I had this persona of an intellectual philosophy student (lol) with a bunch of supporters who'd help me keep my approval rating up. So it was an identity that was constructed, but it still felt authentic – like, it almost felt like an idealised version of what I'd like to be, in a space where nobody was going to judge me for things that were entirely external and beyond my control.'

Though part of me wishes the internet still functioned in such a way, it isn't especially hard to understand why it stopped. Even if we would like them not to, things that are entirely external and beyond our control – Io's accidents of birth and accidents of circumstance – shape who we are. I am who I am not just because of what I think and feel but because I was brought up in France, am a woman from a broadly middle-class background and am an Arab who looks white. I could deny it, but it wouldn't change a thing.

Similarly, Hussein ended up becoming a reporter focusing on British Muslim issues at *BuzzFeed* because he is British and Muslim. Who we are in real life influences who we become in real life; it was only a matter of time before the internet caught up.

As has now become a common refrain, I don't believe you could pinpoint the moment it happened; there was no day online when we collectively took off our masks and revealed ourselves. It is also worth saying that there are still many pockets on the internet where people can choose to reveal very little of themselves, but for the most part, we are now less anonymous than we used to be. Instead of being completely different people across platforms, we are now more or less the same across the internet and everything we do floats closer to the surface. I suppose I could, in theory, develop a new passion and go off in search of people who share that passion with me, but I worry it would not be the same. I may be a slightly different person on Instagram than I am on Twitter or – god forbid – Facebook, but the differences are fairly minimal.

I have recently started playing video games and now tweet about them from the account I use to tweet about everything else. I have no intentions of going out of my way to establish a new persona as a gamer as the people who enjoy gaming are, by and large, on the same platforms I am already on. When once we were on a beach as creatures who could live and hide under different rocks, we now all exist on the same patch of sand, and the rocks are long gone.

It isn't all bad; as Alice reminded me, it is still possible to find your people online today. Still, it doesn't quite feel the same; she is a grown woman and so am I. It is relatively easy for us to have the confidence to throw ourselves into things in full view of everyone else. Would someone younger or less self-assured do the same? Would it still feel as freeing? What would happen if they decided they didn't like the identity they'd created for themselves? Can you still reinvent yourself as thoroughly as we once did?

We were once little crabs hiding under rocks on the beach but the rocks are gone; there were once countless niches on the internet but there are now a few large platforms and we are all on them together. I promised that this book would not be about tech but this is an unavoidable topic – the moment we all joined Facebook, our collective dream began to die. It is something I talked about with Hussein, because I wanted to know what he made of the communities created on today's internet. His outlook was pessimistic and I can't really blame him.

'I think communities can still be created online – there are, for example, minority religious/ethnic/ linguistic communities that exist mainly in digital spaces and they operate as both communal spaces and as archives to enshrine languages that would die out otherwise,' he said. 'But the role of the platform is way more important and powerful – so for example, I know of some communities that centred around old video games, or even old memories of towns during certain time periods, that either got taken over by bots on Facebook, or deleted entirely by Web-hosting platforms that were moving to cloud-based systems or just shuttering.

'Often, the communities involved wouldn't be that tech savvy, so would have no idea what to do to keep their archives/memories/chat logs, etc. By extension, what happens if a community built around relatable moments on Facebook suddenly gets turned into a platform for conspiracies, or if members splinter/go to war with each other, etc.? In this case, the absence of the moderator seems instructive. In *TOTSE*, for example, even though a lot of the material on that site was designed to be crude, crass and obtuse, we all knew who the moderators were and mods would come down hard if you breached any rules of the forum. These days, I don't think people know who their moderators are.

'Tech giants outsource their moderation to algorithms, or centres that screen for behaviour that might be extremist or violent – but they don't really care about the communities they cultivate on their platforms. So even if a Facebook group is 'moderated', it's an alienating process, dehumanised and also just not really all that fun to participate in.'

At the risk of sounding like an inspirational poster, communities are like gardens and need to be tended in order to survive. How people behave in these communities is only one part of the equation; if they are not given the spaces to bloom, there is not much they can do. You can water plants all you want, but with the wrong soil, they will keep withering.

Still, the tension at the very heart of online communities is that the freedom within them is what made them special. We could be whoever we wanted to be and go wherever we wanted to go; being left to our own devices was the whole point. How to square this with the mentally ill kids making each other worse on Tumblr, or the girls telling each other to starve themselves on Instagram? It was not always healthy or safe to find your people on the internet and perhaps that was the point, but perhaps that is why they couldn't quite last.

Communities are like gardens, and if we are not careful they can be overrun by weeds, or so manicured they no longer look like real nature. There is a middle ground to be reached but it is not clear that anyone has really managed it, especially not at scale. *TOTSE* was probably good, but it occurred at a time when the internet was smaller and even then, things could – and did – frequently turn sour.

It worked, just about, because not many people knew or cared about what was going on online at the time. Young teenagers probably should not have been given free rein to that extent and now we know that, there is no turning back. We had something that we probably never should have had and now it is gone.

There are still communities online and they are big and small, good and bad, but they are not quite the same, they never could be. It's a shame because I wish the latecomers to the internet could have experienced what we had, for a brief time, but their very arrival marked the end of the era. We found a home then it was invaded; it was no one's fault, not really, but now everyone is here and our home is gone.

Wind, Guide Me

There was a point in 2016 when I realised that my social life had taken a nosedive. For a while I could not put my finger on what had happened. I still had the same life and the same friends but I was getting invited to fewer things and didn't really know what to do about it.

Eventually I realised what the problem was: I had started using Facebook at 16 and was by that point around 24. I had never known what it was like to go out without always relying on Facebook events. It was an epiphany; thinking back, it hit me that Facebook events were the one thing that had shaped my social life like nothing else.

I would rarely ask anyone but close friends to hang out because I knew that I would be seeing them at some house party a few days later, because they had clicked 'attending' on the event. I did not make plans because instead I could click on the 'events' tab on the day and decide what I wanted to do. There was always something in that tab; a party, a birthday, a club night, a squat rave – everything was happening and I was always welcome.

I could turn up to events alone because I knew that X and Y had clicked 'attending', and, failing that, Z was a 'maybe'. In an odd way, my social life involved very little agency; I knew I wanted to go out all the time, so I just went to whatever I was invited to without questioning it. When Facebook started suggesting events their friends were attending to its users, I also started going to things I was not invited to. I crashed parties and birthdays like there was no tomorrow; if there was a guest list for a gig or a club night, I was on it.

For a while I lived in a cheap and horrible little flat in Shoreditch with a few friends and we had huge parties every month, because there was nothing in that flat that could be broken or stolen. We all invited our entire friends lists and kept the events public. Once, an acquaintance turned up with 17 people he had found outside a club. We let them in.

It was like running your life by rolling a dice; I was a stray cat walking in and out of people's flats and parties, and whoever I met enough times ended up becoming my friend. I didn't choose people and they didn't choose me; we just kept clicking 'attending' on the same things.

It is odd to think about it now; I wonder how much of it had to do with my mostly friendless childhood and the trust issues that came with it. If I did not sincerely try to befriend people, they could not hurt me by turning me down. Instead, I could simply float around and see where the tab would take me next. As a result, the slow demise of Facebook events was both a curse and a blessing; it left a huge hole in my life but forced me to learn how to lead a normal social life. Left without the safety net of endless potential parties, I had to decide who I liked and who I didn't, and how to go about seeing the people whose company I did enjoy.

Still, I'm glad it is something I got to live through; it was a very specific phenomenon and it happened at a very specific time, and I'm not sure what I would have done without it. How else would I have made friends when I moved to London? Without it, would I have ended up befriending the people on my university course? I had nothing against them but I'm pleased I didn't. Instead, going to all these random parties, birthdays, club nights, gigs and raves introduced me to so many people, subcultures and parts of London I would have missed otherwise. They allowed me to meet the coolest people in town and realise that they were not very fun after all; they made me realise I could socialise with just about anyone if I wanted to and that I was pretty good at it.

Intellectually, I know that making my social life smaller and more deliberate was a good thing overall, but I do sometimes wish that Facebook events never went out of fashion. There really was magic in that tab. Still, that it was such a transient phase is entirely the point. It is why I really wanted to mention it here; it may seem like a small thing but it really encapsulates the point of this book and explains what I mean when I talk about growing up online. If you were not of a certain age and of a certain disposition at a certain point, this probably passed you by.

The internet is more stuck in its ways now than it ever was. There may be trends and new features occasionally added to apps but the fundamentals do not change in the way they used to. In 2006, I had a blog and I talked to friends on MSN and made new ones on MySpace and I could only be online when I was at home.

Five years later, I no longer had a blog and no longer used MSN or MySpace but was instead on Facebook and Instagram and Twitter, and I checked all three of them everywhere on my smartphone. Ten yeas after that, I was still primarily on Facebook and Instagram and Twitter, and still checked all three of them everywhere on my smartphone. Some things have changed – I use WhatsApp, my phone camera takes better selfies – but, in a more concrete sense, not much has changed at all.

Technology has not evolved dramatically and my everyday life online has stagnated for a long time now. Facebook events were special because they were, in retrospect, ephemeral. They took over my social calendar for six or seven years then disappeared, and were not replaced by anything.

My life shifted because I took a very liberal attitude to adding friends on Facebook from 2008 onwards and I wanted to party all the time. Things aligned in exactly the right way and here I am today. Things were good but they didn't last – or perhaps things were good because we knew they couldn't last. What happens when so much of the internet now feels like it could last forever?

More Than a Woman

One of my earliest vivid memories is of school, when I was seven. I had just skipped a year which, coupled with the fact that I was born in December, meant that I was two years younger than everyone else. I was talking to my grandmother after she'd come to pick me up and I told her, in an exasperated tone, that all the girls in my class were boring. All they wanted to do was talk about nail varnish and boys and I didn't want to talk about either of those things. The boys were boring too, because I wanted to play with them and they didn't want to play with me.

It is not an especially remarkable memory, and isn't even the earliest I have; instead, I remember it well because I do not merely remember the sequence of events, but the strength of my exasperation. If I stop and think about it for a few minutes, I can be transported back to that living room, physically seething at the dullness of nail varnish and boys.

It is probably no surprise that, as a result, I later became one of those teenage girls then women who was one of the lads, always hanging out with the boys, not your typical gal, and so forth. It is an embarrassing admission to make now, because the wind has turned and female friendships are now seen as the single best part of being human, but I really can't help it. Even today, I can go out for six nights in a row then, on the Sunday, realise that in that time I only saw one or two women. For whatever reason, I have always found it easier to befriend men.

Imagine my surprise, then, when I started research-ing this book and drew up a list of the people I wanted to interview. The idea, as outlined earlier, was to try and talk to the people who had shaped my online life between roughly 2005 and 2020. The final tally included 30 names; of those, only eight were men. This was an issue; the thesis I had prepared for this essay was based on the idea that, in life as online, I had always surrounded myself with men. Had I not? This is when I realised that I had managed to Rule 16 myself.

If you're lucky enough not to know what this means, Rule 16 means that 'there are no girls on the internet'. As *Urban Dictionary* puts it:

'Expanded Rule 16 states that:

a) All internet men are men

b) All internet women are really men

c) All internet children are policemen'

It is all obviously a bit of a joke, but there is an element of truth in there. Growing up online as a woman was an odd experience and involved spending a lot of time assuming – not incorrectly – that you were the exception. It isn't that there weren't any women involved; we just knew the spaces we were in had not been designed with us in mind.

The rules were not made with us in mind and the coarse and rude sense of humour that was pervasive at the time had clearly been cultivated by young men. I spent those years making 'edgy' sexist jokes because everyone around me online made them and so I assumed they were the done thing.

Offline perceptions of the internet shaped this culture as well; until the early 2010s, the image of the computer geek was a distinctly male one. People chained to their computers in the noughties were generally assumed to be men, usually white, almost certainly single and not especially pleasant-looking.

It was a bit of a chicken-and-egg situation: was the early internet shaped by people who weren't very good at real life because they had no other choice, or did people who could have been halfway decent at real life end up becoming secluded because they spent too much time on the early internet? It was a little bit of column A and column B, presumably; in any case, by the time I arrived in the early 00s, Rule 16 was in full swing.

At the same time, the rise of MSN Messenger meant that hormone-fuelled teens and tweens had more access than ever to the boys – or girls, or both – that they yearned for. MSN proto-flirting became a part of all our lives; I cannot count the number of times it came up in conversations with interviewees for this book.

'As a teenager, I do remember spending hours on MSN Messenger, chatting to my school friends and to boys,' author Otegha Uwagba told me. 'Boys were a scarce commodity because I went to a girls' school, so it was boys from the local boys' school. I would chat with my friends quite a bit but also it would be quite gossipy; you'd have a fight with someone or be sent copied and pasted transcript of somebody else's chat, or have a conversation with a boy and then tell your friends about it afterwards, making it sound like it was much more than it was.'

We all have our war stories, but the single most embarrassing example I can think of involved a boy I will not name. I was about 14 and overflowing with lust; he was 16 and – naturally, given his advanced age – mature and aloof. We talked on MSN every other evening, having met through our music blogs.

One night, for reasons now lost to both history and shame, I decided to make good use of my grainy, shoddy webcam to show him some of my most stylish (and flattering) outfits. I'd come up with a pretext so flimsy I cannot remember it now and twirled in front of my camera as he typed wry comments in the chat.

Eventually, he told me that the entire thing had been an embarrassment, that I had clearly been vying for his attention, but that he forgave me because I was only 14. Believe me when I tell you that typing this, 15 years later, still makes my chest tighten. It is the first time I have ever mentioned the incident to anyone.

I'm not telling this story out of sheer masochism; I brought it up because it was an especially egregious example of a dynamic that has dominated my entire life online. The internet reached a recognisable form at the point at which my peers and I were teeming with hormones and desperate to be noticed by just about any boy (or girl, or both). There were atrocious attempts at flirting on MSN and minor heart attacks when someone commented on your MySpace profile picture; vague and gloomy screen names after disappointing conversations and bathroom selfies taken at unreasonable angles.

I kissed my first boy on a summer holiday at 12 then

we talked on MSN every day for weeks because he had fallen for me and I wanted to be polite. Between the ages of 15 and 17, I ended up in the odd situation of repeatedly trying and failing to snog boys from my high school and so instead snogging boys from indie bands I'd interviewed for my blog.

It was, in retrospect, hilarious. My seduction skills in person were so poor that I could not get into the pants of any of the spotty 16-year-olds I coveted. Music journalist and 'recently turned 18, actually' Margaret, on the other hand, got off with people still too famous to mention here. I led a deeply absurd double life and it was delightful.

I'm happy to admit that I was an edge case, but my intentions remained the same as everyone else; I was given a tool which could facilitate the sticking of my tongue in some boys' mouths and I held on to it for dear life. This was, in a way, the unintended consequence of Rule 16: if you were going to put all these men into one space, voracious young women were always going to follow. That said, an interesting feature I had not really noticed at the time but which now seems obvious is that the internet was, at the time, fairly gendered.

We had some demilitarised zones, where boys and girls could meet and attempt to smoothly interact with one another, but ultimately, there were many corners of the internet that were inherently female.

Most of the people I interviewed for this were women because, in retrospect, most of my early internet was women. There were blogs written by girls oversharing about their mundane lives; fashion bloggers turning clothes they'd found in skips into awe-inspiring outfits; streetstyle blogs that felt like wanderlust; and sex writers teaching us trade secrets.

I had grown up finding girls weird, boring and scary but suddenly I'd found all these other teenagers who thought and dressed and wrote like me and it was a revelation. As Tea told me, 'It felt like I was part of a movement and I felt like for the first time ... not to be cheesy, but I was really connected to all these other girls my age, from all around the world. I'd literally never, ever experienced something like that, which now to kids on Instagram and TikTok seems normal, but it wasn't normal: it was the first time ever we were able to do that.'

Crucially, I do also believe that we, wayward and maladjusted young women that we were, played a crucial part in shaping the internet that we know and (sometimes) love today. From oversharing and selfies to pointless bitch fights and aesthetically pleasing web pages, the influence of teenage girls is everywhere you look, even today.

Boys had their crude jokes and flame wars but we spent hours working out how to take the best mirror selfies and spilling our guts and feelings into our blogs. We compulsively shared banal updates about our day and we would always call out those who had wronged us, but never by name. We invented it all. In return, the early internet shaped us as well; I know so many women who never would have turned to feminism if they had stayed offline. Women's mags and mainstream television did not bring us up; instead, we learned from each other and from our elders, who were by then in their early to mid-twenties.

It was a messy process; the online feminism of 2007 was not the online feminism of 2010, and the online feminism of 2012 was so different from the feminism of 2018 that they may as well be entirely different movements.

I exaggerate, of course, but only slightly. One example I always enjoy is #KillAllMen, and the many troubles of ironic misandry. I first encountered it on Tumblr – where else? – in 2012 or 2013. The feminism of the era was edgy and performatively violent; think 'may the wings of your eyeliner be so sharp they could kill a man', and semi-erotic pictures of thin women posing with large knives.

#KillAllMen was not meant to be taken seriously but it was everywhere; you could use it as a standalone statement or at the end of a whinge about your male housemate finishing the communal shampoo. It wasn't even a slogan anymore; after a while, it read as punctuation. It wasn't entirely uncontroversial but, when challenged, the women who used it claimed that the universality of it was the entire point.

When men started arguing that, well, not all men were dreadful, the hashtag #NotAllMen was hastily deployed and the case was closed. Things got dicy when the political discourse turned to police violence against black and brown men in the US. Suddenly, #KillAllMen started to look quite tactless. It was soon replaced by #KillAllWhiteMen, to make it clear that wry feminists were not siding with racist police forces everywhere.

Because the dam had now broken, conversations were had on where exactly trans men fitted into the whole thing, given that suicide rates among the trans community are – tragically – sky-high. #KillAllCisWhiteMen was proposed as an alternative, but it just wasn't that catchy anymore. By around 2016, the hashtag, in all its forms, had more or less disappeared; men lived to see another day.

These years felt odd. Young women who had spent their teenage years online were acutely aware of the fact that the young men who had spent their teenage years online largely hated them. As in society at large, sexist jokes and a general stench of misogyny had permeated the internet for a long time; this violent misandry felt like a sometimes ironic, sometimes helpless comeback. Men hated us so we decided to hate them even more.

It also felt like a coping mechanism. I remember being in the pub one evening in 2012 with some female friends; an old and crass regular made a crude pass at one of us and she burst out crying. Online, she had been the sort of person who'd post memes about gangs of feminist vigilantes stalking the streets with baseball bats; in person, a light bit of catcalling made her crumble.

I felt quite sorry for her at the time; after the pub incident, I started seeing her online posturing in a different light. For some, online misandry was a pastime like any other; for others, a way to work around their trauma. In any case, this mini wave – wavelet? ripple? – of feminism did not last for very long. I wonder if it is because we got older and learned that nuance could sometimes be useful. Many men hurt women but, at risk of giving credence to irritating trolls, not all of them do. Alienating men who could fall either way helps no one.

It also helped that some women showed us a better way. One of them was Madeleine Holden, who was behind the blog *Critique My Dick Pic*. It was, for a long time, one of my favourite websites, despite being little more than an avalanche of penises.

If you never came across it, *CMDP* very much did what it said on the tin: men could send in anonymous pictures of their genitals and Madeleine – who was then anonymous – would advise them on angles, lighting, background, grip and so on. As the site's description made clear, she decided very early on never to critique the actual penises, their girth, length or general appearance. Instead, she merely offered notes on whether the pictures were any good.

'I noticed that there were two main problems with dick pics: one is that they're so often sent unsolicited, and another is that they're almost always of terrible artistic quality,' she told me in an email. 'In 2013, I received a welcome, high-quality dick pic in my personal life and was joking with my friends about how rare that is and how we needed to set up some kind of public service to guide men in this area. I picked up the joke and ran with it, and started *CMDP* on Tumblr that same afternoon.

'It blew up really quickly: the website *Jezebel* named it the Tumblr of the Week about three days after I launched it and it got quite a bit of interest in mainstream publications.'

In a way, *CMDP* had it all; there were titillating pictures taken by masters of their craft, grossly funny and grainy pictures of penises taken from above ('the log', as she came to call this type of shot) and gently encouraging comments, politely telling senders what they had done wrong and offering them to try again and send in an updated picture.

'I'm happy with the tone and approach I took: at the time, the "snarky" blog tone was still quite dominant and I think it would have been easy to do a version of *CMDP* where I told men their dicks were trash, rah rah rah, don't waste my time, etc.,' Madeleine wrote. 'That kind of nail-polish-emoji sassiness was big back then and there was a lot of demand for it. I ended up going for something more earnest, pedagogical and encouraging—the tone was like a teacher grading homework—and I think it aged better because of that.'

In the oasis that was the website of dick pics, men also acted quite pleasantly: 'I was always surprised by how little harassment I received. There was one guy who sent me a video where he was masturbating to a picture of my face he'd found on my social media, and there were a few guys who were a bit persistent in sending submissions, but these were isolated incidents among literally thousands and thousands of submissions, and senders were, on the whole, very well behaved.'

ESCAPE

This is, I think, because there are a lot of men who only really want one thing from the internet: the attention and respect of women who they consider to be superior to them in some way. In Madeleine's case, her status came from her kind but firm advice on the topic of erect penises.

To oversimplify: there are millions of men online who are, at any given point, 14-year-old Marie twirling in a vintage skirt in front of a grainy webcam for a 16-year-old boy. It is not an entirely online phenomenon, of course, but on the internet these men rise and fall as waves and it is easier to spot the patterns.

We often call them 'reply guys' because replying to the tweets women post is seemingly all they ever do. They can be entirely harmless or creepily desperate; actually interesting or uncomfortably overfamiliar. The tone of their replies can be patronising, helpful, jokingly insulting or amusingly deferential. What they all have in common is that their words mean little and what they're clearly typing is 'me! me! pick me! pick me!' Every woman with even a hint of a profile on the internet will have a handful of them; reply guys have become a part of life.

An especially odd aspect of this phenomenon is that, if you are a young woman with even a hint of a profile on the internet, men will often want to send you money. I'm not entirely sure when it became the (literal) currency of these social interactions, but I would guess that *Patreon* had something to do with it.

The platform allows content creators to get money from their fans and followers so they can produce some drawings, essays, or whatever else they are known for. It was launched in 2013 and became popular among freelance writers a few years later. I remember it well because I remember noticing that only young women I knew were joining it.

The main reason for this may well be that it was harder for these young women to progress in newsrooms in the same way their male counterparts did. Still, the gendered nature of it was hard to avoid. Because of the way *Patreon* works, one must offer rewards in exchange for different amounts of money – give me five dollars a month and I'll do X, ten and I'll throw in Y as well, and so on.

Often, what these women would offer were promises of email exchanges about their work; for the highest tiers, they would even Skype with you to discuss story ideas. I looked through their subscribers at the time and the overwhelming majority of them were men. What they were offering was, in essence, a girlfriend experience; chuck me 20 quid a month and I'll pretend that I love talking to you. Give me a little more and you'll be able to see my face, and, if you're lucky, the inside of my bedroom.

I'm not naming these women – some of whom you may have heard of, some of whom you almost certainly have not – because I have no idea if they knew what they were doing and I didn't want to ask them. Did they realise these sweaty men so obviously would not have cared about their writing if they had been older or less conventionally attractive? Did they care? Did they, on some level, enjoy the attention? Can you imagine asking this of one of your friends? I am a coward and so I did not.

It is also not about them, not really. There are so many men online who want to give money to women. I have received so many direct messages from random, usually polite men offering to fund my lifestyle: 'I just really love your writing,' they would tell me, 'and it doesn't hurt that you look the way you do!' I'd wince and close the tab.

In one of the lockdowns I had no money and I was very sad, and I wanted a pizza from Domino's. I'd recently written some fun blog posts for free and so I tweeted a link to one of those apps that allow you to send money to a stranger. 'If you enjoyed my blogs, do consider throwing a couple of quid in my general direction!' I tweeted.

In about 15 minutes I'd received over 100 pounds – only nine of those had come from a woman. Men had sent me over 100 pounds in about 15 minutes. In a panic, I deleted the tweet and felt gross. I ordered my pizza and, with the leftover money, bought some furniture for my flat.

I've often wondered if I should embrace this dynamic instead; men in my life have frequently told me I should do it. They find it very amusing that being a vaguely decent-looking woman online means that men want to send you money. Why shouldn't you take it? What they do not understand is that it feels, at heart, like a hostile act. Men who want to send money to women for no obvious reason are nothing but a reminder of Rule 16. They want to make us feel special and, by doing so, they remind us – or me, at least – that the internet is not our natural home.

We are special guests and it's nice to have us here, but our presence cannot ever be neutral because we do not really belong. Really, I would rather just be left alone. I would also like the internet to go back to the way it used to be, which is very small and petty of me. I liked it when being a woman online meant that you were probably a bit weird and different. It sounds insufferable written down but there is no point in denying it.

I realised this when I talked about this with a friend and we tried to pinpoint the moment at which the internet stopped feeling like it was ours. It was – don't laugh – when conventionally attractive people became very popular online.

I'd never thought about it until that conversation and it felt like a lightbulb moment. It didn't quite happen when webcams and smartphones joined the equation; even then, weird and quirky fashion on weird and quirky people dominated for a while. MySpace hardly was a repository for mainstream hotness either, as all former emos will be able to tell you.

Perhaps Instagram was the beginning of the end, then; the moment when thin white women with long hair and men with lean abs and square jaws came to dominate our lives again. I'm aware that this makes me sound like an incel, but I do not resent those people, not really; it is not their fault that they are very beautiful. They should enjoy having the faces and bodies that they do.

I suppose what I find irksome, despite my best efforts, is that it is our haven that they invaded. They are not the problem but their presence is. There are still pockets of people online who are funnier than they are pretty but we do not make the rules anymore. I hate that I am writing this, it makes me feel small and like a gloomy teenager, but here we are.

Everywhere I look online there are women doing make-up tutorials and they bore me to death. I escaped to the internet because I didn't want to listen to girls talk about make-up and 20 years later, they are haunting me again. It is not a fashionable view to hold because all of the girls and all of the boys are online now, and girls sniping at other girls is frowned upon.

Or maybe it isn't anymore. There have been so many waves of feminism and ways of being a woman in the past few years that I have lost track. For a while we were all supposed to want to have long hair and wear high heels and red lipstick but only ever for us and never for men. We were told we should be going for high-profile and ludicrously well-paid jobs, even though they sound exhausting and most women do not want or cannot have those. We were meant to support those who followed that path, though, because that is what women did to one another. No woman could ever do anything wrong. Everything was good and feminist; existing as a woman was, in itself, an act of feminism.

That entire way of thinking collapsed in, oh, 2016? 2017? and finally, it was okay to criticise women again, but it was not clear what they could be criticised for. Were strippers the devil or were the women who publicly hated strippers? Was deciding to look feminine a way to show that you had capitulated to men or a sign that you were your own person? Were careers good or bad? Kids? Sleeping with men? Ad nauseam.

Interestingly, this triggered something of an identity crisis among men as well. Were they individually responsible for all the evils of the world? If not, who was? Could you be masculine without being toxic? Was there such a thing as masculinity anyway? How should they interact with women, online and in real life? Can straight male lust ever be expressed in an acceptable fashion?

A lot of these questions floated around but were never quite answered. Similarly, men worried about their mental health problems and higher risk of suicide but no one quite knew what to do about them. How does class interact with masculinity? How does race? The discussions were everywhere and nowhere at the same time, bubbling up on occasion but never filling the mainstream.

Young men wanted to be different from the generations that came before them but did not really know what they meant by that. What role models could they turn to? Is acknowledging problematic behaviour then engaging in that same behaviour yourself even worse than doing so without realising? Some men adopted the clothing and the words of soft and progressive subcultures, then used them to make the old, toxic ways more palatable.

Men were told to call each other out when needed but did not always have the words to do so. They were told to do something – anything – to help women and ease their burden, and they were told off for talking over them. It was agreed that a change was needed but neither men nor women could decide how they should proceed.

In short, there were no longer set ways in which to be a man or a woman online. Men on the internet were the men of real life and the women were as well. Everyone boring and normal is here now and so we interact in ways that are largely normal and often boring. Beautiful people are popular because they were always going to be; the weirdos feel left out from mainstream culture because they always do. Men want to send money to women because they can no longer buy them drinks in bars; feminists argue about feminism all the time because it is what we do. The platforms we are on are so large that we must cohabit most of the time; like housemates, we have our corners but are ultimately stuck under the same roof.

I once felt that being online was more important to my personality than being a woman; I've never been hugely attached to my gender anyway. I resent that everyone is here now and that it means that I have lost a side of myself. I was bad at being a girl in real life, so instead I became a girl on the internet.

I am really only just a normal woman now, and isn't that boring?

A/S/L?

It is my sincere belief that dating apps were a victory of the Not Very Online against us, the Very Online. It isn't exactly a thesis, more of a gut feeling. Well, either that or the defence mechanism of a wounded ego.

I managed to write an entire proposal for this book – an endeavour that took many weeks – and not once did it occur to me to include apps in my pitch. It was not a conscious decision, and it was only halfway through writing that last chapter that I realised something was very obviously missing.

I was writing about people using the internet to try and get laid and somehow I hadn't thought to mention the main way in which they have been doing so –'glaring' doesn't begin to cover it. As I see it, there are several reasons for this. The first one is that, as stated above, I do not consider dating apps to be an especially 'online' part of the internet. (I realise this sentence makes no sense in and of itself but if you've read this far then you know what I mean, don't you? I really hope you do. I've been doing a very bad job otherwise.)

As a number of their ads have snappily put it, their ultimate goal is to become redundant. Apps like *Tinder* and *Bumble* do not exist to be downloaded and kept forever; they are liminal spaces, like bus stops or doctors' waiting rooms. You come in, do what you have to do, leave again. On top of that, the point of these apps is to facilitate the meeting of people in person. They are, ultimately, a tool that happens to have found the internet as a home. That is the first reason why I dislike them – they have taken my world and used it for their convenience.

The second is that I am appallingly, embarrassingly bad at dating apps. I have been on *OKCupid*, *Tinder*, *Bumble* and *Hinge* and not once have I managed to meet someone from any of these apps. I have swiped the right way on hundreds of people and, at most, a few dozens swiped back. Of those, none turned into a date. It is both mortifying and fascinating. I know that the issue is not me, not really; I have dated many people in the past 15 years or so, and have faith in my ability to charm strangers and acquaintances alike if I really want to. Of those strangers and acquaintances, a majority were met through blogs, or Twitter after that; I have slid into numerous DMs and, more often than not, managed to take that to its natural conclusion.

Why, then, am I so comically bad at chatting people up in the very places you go to in order to chat people up? Here's my theory: the apps were created at a stage of the internet when everyone had already joined in, and are consequently ruled by the sense of etiquette of the less online among us. The sense of humour is different and so is the tone; the difference is hard to explain but easy to see once you encounter it, a bit like when the air changes as it's about to rain.

More importantly, the way to stand out on dating apps is to look and sound like everyone else. I have swiped on my accounts and I have swiped on the accounts of friends; I have seen men and women who all looked the same and talked about the same things, professed to have the same interests and made the same jokes. The internet was once a haven for individuality but the only way to get laid on Tinder is to look like you could be anyone. The blander your quips, the more attractive you become; it is a numbers game and you can only win it by turning yourself into the lowest common denominator. It is the opposite of what we came online to do and it is hell.

On a more personal note, I would also argue that the

flirting there is never truly flirting, because it is assumed from the very start that flirting is about to happen.

Hitting on someone is at its most fun when it is at least a little bit transgressive. It's about the looks you throw at someone or the words you use to talk about something; more importantly, it is about making your intentions clear enough without making them overly obvious. It's especially entertaining to do online because you cannot see the person and, if your approach is being made on Twitter or elsewhere, you cannot be too upfront. The only thing you can play with is your tone, the words you use and the frequency at which you send your messages. You can also shape and contort your entire online presence for a while, knowing deep down that you are doing it for an audience of one. There can be jokes about topics that you know the person whose attention you crave cares about; there can be flattering posted when you know they will be looking. The flirting can also happen across different platforms, as well as publicly and in private. There can be light mocking on the timeline, then more earnest discussions in DMs, or vice versa.

There is also some (light) stalking, of course; if someone cannot pull up a person's entire life story from their first name and the place they were born, did they really grow up online? From old social media profiles or stray links, one can gain better insights into the other person's tastes in music, clothes, books or whatever else; the more you know about someone, the easier it is to guess what will make them tick.

I'm sure it must have felt creepy at the beginning, or for those older than us; because I have never known anything else, I would find the opposite bewildering. Did people really used to decide they fancied someone based on incomplete information? What a bizarre thing to do. Instead, the uncertainty of online flirting comes from the very nature of both parties' intentions. I have, on numerous occasions, gone for drinks with people I met on Twitter without knowing if the drinks were friendly, a date, professional networking or a combination of all of the above.

It has sometimes been disappointing, embarrassing or both; no one wants to turn up to what clearly feels like a work drink while wearing an especially revealing dress. Most of the time, however, it has been wonderful: if you play your cards right, there is nothing as fun as excited uncertainty. Did you both agree to meet for the same reasons? If not, can your motives evolve as the evening goes on? Will the chemistry you clearly had online still exist in person? If not, who will be the first to bow out politely? If so, who will make the first move? And so on. In a way, turning up is the easiest thing; predicting whether you will leave with a new lover, friend or contact is quite another.

In comparison, dating apps can only ever be ragingly dull. Everyone who is on there is on there for the same reasons and the only difference is between the people who would like to have sex and leave it at that and the ones who would rather find someone they can have sex with until death does them part. Ideally, both parties have already made their intentions clear during the initial online conversations; more often than not, they even state those goals and preferences in their profile. How is that not boring? I don't think I will ever understand it.

On the bright side, I suppose that dating apps' ever-growing popularity have sorted us single people into two categories: those who would use them and those who would not. That's a good thing, because my brief forays into them showed me that there was no one for me there. Instead, I will merrily go back to liking and replying to people's tweets enough that they notice me but not so much that it is clear that I probably fancy them. It's childish and time-consuming but I do believe it's the only way I will meet someone I genuinely like. I have tried dating people who were not very online before and it didn't go well; they didn't get any of my cultural references and our senses of humour were just too different.

I suppose I could submit myself to the thrice-daily 'hey :)' from a 31-year-old accountant who doesn't understand memes, but I'm not sure it would ever help me or them. Dating apps are for people who see the internet as an extension of real life, which I simply refuse to accept. They may be right, but that doesn't mean I'm ready to give up on my ways just yet.

XX Sex

Where were you the first time you watched a video of a woman getting fucked with a frozen trout? I was at home in my bedroom and I was 12. Some boys and I had started a contest in which we had to find the weirdest piece of porn on the internet. Because it was 2004, it felt like a reasonable endeavour.

Our favourite video ended up being one of a woman kneeling and giving head to a group of men all dressed like pterodactyls from the waist up. Yes, there were wings and yes, they made dinosaur sounds. I eventually won the contest by finding and watching a video of a man fucking the eye socket of a rotting sheep's head. I had, by that point, only ever kissed one boy, without tongues. This is why older people make me laugh when they say they worry about the young watching sex online that doesn't look like the sort of sex people actually have – they don't know the half of it.

Porn has been a part of my life for as long as I can remember. Because we grew up in a nerdy household, my brother and I were early adopters of peer-to-peer file sharing, where every movie might be a woman getting gangbanged and every TV series episode a close-up of a blowjob. We even joked about it together; when a file finished downloading, we'd open it together then frantically close the tab if needed, laughing hysterically. From memory, there was only ever a 50/50 chance that a movie turned out to actually be what it'd advertised.

There were pop-ups as well; endless breasts appearing on the screen, no matter what you did or which sites you visited. Flesh was, in those years, unavoidable. It was also exceptionally easy to find once we decided that, actually, we did want to see some of it. Like many women my age, the first erect penis I saw was on one of those sites – a French one, I can't remember what it was called – where we could speak to strangers.

'We' in this case always represented a group of just-about-pubescent girls, aged 12 or 13 and attending a sleepover. We would pretend to be 19 or 21 and we would talk to men and tell them we wanted to have cyber sex with them. We were all virgins, of course, so we could competently handle the kissing and the fondling but had no idea what to say once the clothes were off.

I remember once having cybersex with a man in a lift – we'd been making out passionately – but when he wrote that he was sticking his tongue inside my vagina I felt a wave of disgust wash over me and closed the window. Still, most of the time we would ask the man to turn on his webcam and, invariably, we would watch a grainy penis being handled on the screen for about 30 seconds before deciding it was too much.

It was both disgusting and intensely compelling, as early sex often turns out to be. It is also odd to think about today. The adult in me wants to think that these young girls were being preyed on by grown men who knew exactly who they were showing their penises to; the former young girl in me thought it was very fun. I also do not feel traumatised by it in any way; there is a ravenous curiosity that comes with hormones beginning to fill your body and we merely ran with them. It was fun and absurd and I never felt threatened by any of it.

Girl On The Net had a similar experience – a woman in her mid-thirties and an anonymous sex blogger, her introducion to sex came from the internet: 'I remember at school occasionally being allowed on the open internet, and getting super-excited with my friends that we could access chatrooms,' she told me in an email. 'Talking to total strangers via the anonymity of a chat box felt like the most thrilling thing. The kinds of things that these days I roll my eyes at – like men who just want to turn every conversation to sex – were, in those days, the height of excitement. Tommy, 24, Birmingham wanted to know what colour my eyes were? The JOY! The THRILL!

'I remember once getting myself into huge trouble because I (pretending to be F/19/Portsmouth, actually more like F/14/Portsmouth) got into a lovely chat with a gentleman and gave him my literal phone number. Ten minutes later, when I'd hung up the internet (like you had to do in those days), the home phone rang and my mum told me there was a call for me. I was absolutely terrified. Luckily for me, the guy I was speaking to very swiftly realised I was not as old as I'd claimed to be and he said a very polite goodbye.'

GOTN grew up to be – by her own admission – a massive pervert, and I became someone obsessed with massive perverts. It wasn't that I was obsessed with sex; instead, I couldn't stop reading the blogs of those who were.

There was Candy's secret blog and there were others, now lost to time and the online ether, publishing endless accounts of first person filth.

Then there was Tea and her *Sugar Tits* blog, which

had the added thrill of being anonymous, though I had guessed early on that she was behind it. She has since deleted it so I sadly cannot go through it now to jog my memory. I suppose I could use Wayback Machine to see if it was ever archived but that would feel like an intrusion. Deleting an entire blog is a radical act and one that should be respected.

One person who wouldn't mind me discussing their sex life at length, on the other hand, is Cliff. A trans man, Cliff ran a sex blog called *The Pervocracy*, which he updated regularly from 2007 to 2014. This was (part of) the first entry:

'I'm really unqualified to have a sex blog. I am not:
a) An industry insider. The most I've ever been paid for sex was a half-empty bottle of Bacardi 151. Not that it wasn't damn good rum, but I'm pretty sure that doesn't put me in a position to be a 'proud sacred harlot' or whatnot
or
b) Wildly sexually experienced. I've been with about five guys and one girl, counting one-night stands. Actual relationships: two guys. Never been in an orgy or even a "party", never had or been an erotic slave, never even taken it up the ass, which I believe kindergarteners are doing these days. Their parents think it's 'cute'.

However, I am:

a) Honest and open to the point of compulsion and

b) Relentlessly, voraciously horny.'

Cliff was 21 at that point and had not come out as trans yet. In the first few entries, he wrote about the sex he was having with the men he was dating – some kinkier than others. He eventually decided to go out with the kinkiest man of the lot and the slope got slippery.

Slowly but surely, Cliff's blog became a blog about BDSM. There were harsh beatings, blood, clamps, deep bruises, choking, restraints, safe words and everything else. It wasn't a world I had ever had an interest in, but it was gripping; he wrote openly and deftly about something few people will ever experience.

I'd recommend making sure that no one is looking over your shoulder at this stage, but this is an extract from one of the entries, to give you an idea of what his blog was like:

'Clothespins. One on each nipple, more grabbing up little pinches of the meat of my breasts, and – I yelped with each one – more dangling in two neat rows from my cunt. He teased and twiddled them, flicked and tugged at them, and watched me squirm. He tapped the juncture of the clothespins and my skin with the tip of a cane, and I more than squirmed. He ripped the clothespins off, one by one, and made me count them with my voice muffled through the gag. I was in pain in sensitive places and I couldn't speak or move. I felt so free.'

Though – to be blunt – I was never really aroused by his writing, it remained fascinating. It wasn't just about the pain; BDSM, as he explained well, was as psychological as it was physical. It could also be fun; as an experienced practitioner, he took to trying out *Cosmopolitan*'s 'rough sex' tips – including light bondage with toilet paper – and even wrote a readalong of *50 Shades of Grey*.

I read it all avidly and didn't mind when the blog became about more than sex. After a while, Cliff started writing about his personal life, his gender identity, his relationships more broadly and whatever else he fancied discussing. A lot of it applied to people who weren't into BDSM; there is a post from 2014 I still think about, in which he wrote:

'Maybe the biggest unexpected way kink has improved my life is that I've learned different and much better ways of looking at consent. Because while kink definitely isn't a magical consent haven, the kink community has popularized some pretty cool concepts around negotiation, safewords, limits, the idea that agreeing to one thing is not agreeing to everything, and the idea that who you are does not imply what you're willing to do.

Even when I'm not doing kink, these are useful. It's helped me to structure my statements about what I want based on what I want, not on what I think I'm allowed to ask for. It's helped me put trust in my own limits. I have not purchased an extended warranty since I started doing kink.'

It feels like heavy-handed irony, but following a blog about having the shit kicked out of you for sexual gratification felt like a healthier sexual education than following mainstream culture at the time. The late noughties and early 2010s were still a time when rape jokes and ambient misogyny were everywhere; having a semi-professional masochist teach me about consent was, oddly, better.

What I especially like about *The Pervocracy* is that reading it helped me grow up but, as I later found out, it helped Cliff as well. Though he stopped posting on Blogspot in 2014, I kept following him on Tumblr then Twitter as I had grown attached to his online presence. We talked a few times throughout the years and, when I realised I was going to be writing about his blog, I reached out to him.

'I don't know if I ever would have discovered the organised BDSM scene without the internet. I still would have been kinky in my private life – I was kinky before I knew the name for it, just ask my first boyfriend – but if it weren't for the internet I wouldn't have known there was a community and a sort of theoretical framework for kink,' he told me in an email. 'I could invent spanking on my own; I couldn't invent play parties, safewords, the fine distinctions between top and dominant, and all the rest of it. Without learning what was possible in private, I don't know if I ever would have found a way to practice it in public.'

Still, kink was only ever one part of his life; in a way, writing about it was just as transformative. The real reason I wanted to speak to him was that I couldn't stop thinking about the last ever post he had written on *The Pervocracy*. Though I find it easier to look back at the blog with fondness, those years of his life had clearly been tough. He was struggling with his gender identity, had a complicated relationship with his family and suffered abuse at the hands of a partner.

I know all this because he shared all of it at the time. Had he followed a predictable character arc, his last act should have been one of redemption, realising he'd wanted to be hurt by others because he'd been hurting all along, or something along those lines – 'Now I'm better and I realise I don't need to get flogged then write about it to strangers to feel whole', or whatever.

Instead, this was the last post:

'In retrospect, there were some unhealthy things that drove me to have sex, often violent and risky, with several dozen people and post all about it on the public Internet.

Also in retrospect, this turned out to be a really good plan that vastly improved my life.

I don't think that's how this story is supposed to go. I'm supposed to say something like "I now realize I did these things because as a person who struggled with self-esteem and body image, I wanted to feel desirable," but my feeling is more along the lines of "I wanted to feel desirable, and fuck, it worked." It worked great. Made me feel like the sexiest fat little weirdo on Earth. 100% recommended. Just use a condom.

I wanted to silence some inner pain by blotting it out with physical sensation, and that was a fine decision. It was a Band-Aid on the problem, which is a great metaphor because Band-Aids make you feel better and help you heal. Kink helped me wean off self-harm and it put me in touch with people who were knowledgeable about gender, sexuality, and mental health.'

I wanted to know if he still felt like that seven years later and this is what he told me: 'I said "no regrets" and I meant it – *The Pervocracy* only changed my life for the better. And I've heard from a lot of people, and I still sometimes do, that it changed their life for the better, that it changed how they thought about sex and relationships. I'm not sure how I got there from telling the internet that I really, really like sex but I'm so glad I did. If I had it all to do again, I absolutely would.'

Isn't that neat?

I'm biased, obviously, since I'm one of the people he's talking about. Still, I remain grateful to Cliff, Girl On The Net, Sugar Tits and the others, because they managed to make sex sound both extremely exciting and deeply normal, which society isn't always very good at.

If you grew up as a woman and mostly offline, you were likely told – by your peers, society, authority figures and popular culture – that:

- Sex is something you should care about a lot;
- Sex is not something you, as a woman, should openly want or seek;

- There is such a thing as having too much sex (whore) but also too little sex (frigid fun sponge) and you should always aim to have the right amount of it;
- It is rarely clear what 'the right amount of it' is;
- Sex will almost certainly not be very enjoyable most of the time for you (not for the man, of course);
- You must be good at sex, but not so good that it is suspicious;
- Sex is something that is, in general, done to you, but if it is bad then it is your fault.

I realise that learning about sex from the internet instead was not perfect, but it felt a lot better than this. This is why I bristle when I hear older or less online people discuss the ways in which growing up online can distort one's view of sex entirely. Haven't they seen what it's like out there?

At the very least, my accidental sexual education taught me that women could very well seek sex if they so wished and that consent was never negotiable. It showed me that sex could be done in any way you wanted, as long as you could find someone happy to do it with you. It made me realise I was bisexual and told me that it was fine.

As Girl On The Net pointed out in her email, 'The internet showed people that they are not alone. Got a weird fetish? You're not alone – here's a site where loads of other people who have it get together and chat. Worried about your gender/sexuality feelings? Here are a bunch of qualified experts talking you through things in blog posts, plus forums/sites where you can chat to others who have been through the same thing. Worried about this bit of your body? You're not alone – here are pictures of loads of other people who have this too. It felt so overwhelmingly reassuring.'

Perhaps most importantly, the internet taught me that sex was a normal part of life. It didn't have to be hidden away and only discussed in a hushed, overly excited or judgemental tone. Sex was more or less everywhere online and that was good.

Sadly, it didn't last; as people and corporations flooded our spaces, so did their morals and ways of behaving. A particularly sore point for me was Tumblr banning 'adult content' in 2018, a move mocked at the time because duh, what was anyone else using Tumblr for? That reaction infuriated me because it missed the point entirely. Yes, Tumblr was one of the only remaining mainstream sites that allowed explicit content; no, that didn't mean all we did on there was porn-related.

By 2018, I had been on Tumblr for nearly a decade,

practically making me a community elder. My main blog was one on which I posted beautiful pictures I had come across on my online travels; an 'aesthetics' blog, as we called them at the beginning.

Some of the pictures included nudity; as has art for thousands of years. Still, the vast majority of what I posted was entirely chaste and either pictures of landscapes or especially well-dressed men and women. Some of the blogs I followed also included nudity, but the vast majority did not. There was one sex blog I found amusing, in which a dominant man alternated between posting videos of hardcore porn and thoughtfully answering men's naive and heartfelt questions about love and dating, but he was an exception. For the most part, people posted about sex and they posted about other things; you could scroll through your dashboard and see some memes, earnest discussions on serious topics, gifs of bouncing breasts and pretty pictures of haute couture. It was treated as a topic like any other, because it is – or rather should be – a topic like any other.

By 2018, sexualised nudity had been banned from YouTube, Facebook, Instagram and most other platforms. Tumblr was seen as the exception and therefore a haven for the horny. Though it is true that around a fifth of users had left the platform a year after the rule change, I would argue that the number is much smaller than the original discourse made it seem. To rephrase: around 80 per cent of Tumblr users stayed on post-porn ban.

That's a fair few of us.

Still, the special place we had created for ourselves is now gone. All we have now is this tiered internet, where everything non-sexual can co-exist – including racism, fake news, abuse, misogyny and the like – but nipples are beyond the pale. Though Twitter does still allow adult content on its platform at time of writing, it never quite felt like a safe space for it. I occasionally stumble upon porn videos on there and it feels cold and wrong, like seeing a dick pic staring at you from the page of a newspaper.

By and large, sex on the internet has now become like sex in real life: largely hidden but sort of everywhere, mostly banned but often discussed, and made to feel different from absolutely everything else.

'In some respects, our conversation about sex is opening up and exploding,' Girl On The Net told me. 'If you're branded as "wellness", especially for "female pleasure", then you have tonnes of opportunities. Sex education, too, is getting so much better. At the same time, though, we still have a huge hangup and prudishness about sex that gets in the way of so much of what we do.

'If you're "porn" then you get shadowbanned or

actually banned from many social networks, or you end up in situations where you'll build an audience on a site, then they change their terms and conditions and everything you've worked for is lost. There are myriad tools and promo channels that I'd love to be able to use for my own blog (Google ads to name just one!) but I can't use them because I write about sex.'

Because the contemporary internet is ruled by large companies and the money they want to make from us while preserving their corporate image, sex has once again become something of a taboo. As GOTN points out, applying a veneer of respectability to sex can make it palatable enough to be mainstream, but I resent that it has become a pre-requisite. Sex is something the vast majority of us do and we should be free to discuss and watch it without dressing it up as anything else: 'The problem is that people are simultaneously curious about sex yet also wary of it – "sex" sits in this bucket outside of "normal" life, rather than being acknowledged as part and parcel of most people's lives,' she wrote. 'We have come a long way in tackling the shame and stigma surrounding sex and masturbation, but there's a very long way to go, especially when it comes to porn. Sex can be "educational" or "healthy", but when it's *just plain fucking fun* people get nervous.

'Porn is such a broad genre, and it can be beautiful,

uplifting, weird, quirky, funny, and a whole bunch of stuff. And yeah, it can also be harmful. I'd far rather have a conversation about workers' rights in the adult industry, and how to protect those rights and ensure fair treatment, than have yet another fruitless debate about whether "porn" harms women.'

While I agree with most of this, there is this niggling doubt at the back of my brain. Despite having grown up watching things that no teenage virgin should ever see, my experience with sex-related content online has been, on the whole, a positive one. Still, I can't help but think of a dinner party I had with some friends a few years ago. We were all women and we were all quite drunk; most were around 40 and a few of us were in our twenties. None of the older women had dated in about a decade, which made for an interesting conversation on casual sex.

I couldn't tell you how or why we started discussing choking, but eventually we did. It felt like two alien species meeting each other for the first time. On one side, the older women discussed it as a niche BDSM act; something they had never done and would never want to do, and that felt on par with watersports or nipple clamps.

On the other, my two friends and I explained, plainly, that we had all been choked numerous times by men our age, sometimes because we asked for it and sometimes with no warning, and that we saw it as part and parcel of sleeping with men.

If I were to rank it, I would say it sits somewhere around the light spanking mark; not something that happens every time you have sex with someone, but not so out of the ordinary that you would mention it when describing the experience to someone.

Our older friends were horrified and started looking at us like we were battered women, unaware of the trauma we had suffered. We felt fine; for the most part, we didn't love getting choked but didn't hate it either, just as we didn't love or hate many other things that can happen in a bedroom. In fact, choking had become so mainstream by that point that it was more of a meme than anything else. The first viral post I can remember about it came from Tumblr user mousathe14 in 2015 and it read:

Darth Vader: *force chokes storm trooper*

Storm trooper: harder daddy
Darth Vader: what

Storm trooper: what

A few months before that, KnowYourMeme tells us, 'Gawker published an article titled "The

White House Is Archiving Every Tweet Begging
@POTUS for Sex", which highlighted a tweet sent
to Barack Obama's Twitter feed saying "choke
me daddy."

[...] 'On May 7th, 2017, John Oliver devoted a
majority of his show to explaining the fight over
net neutrality, as well as the plans FCC Chairman
Ajit Pai had for the future of the internet. Oliver
instructed his viewers to comment on the FCC's
website, saying, "And do not tell me that you
don't have time to do this," pointing out various
absurd internet phenomena including those who
tweet "Choke me, daddy" at Pope Francis.'

Tweeting 'choke me daddy' at the Pope had, by
that point, been a done thing for nearly two years; I
remember discussing it with some friends back in
2015. Setting the 'daddy' element aside, the choking
conundrum feels worth exploring.

People having casual sex in their twenties and early
thirties are – anecdotally[1] – more likely to have choked
partners or been choked by them in the past, or are at
the very least comfortable with it as an act. Memes about

---

1   I actually did a Twitter poll on this. It was very unscientific. I will not pretend it would
stand up to academic scrutiny. Still, out of a panel of 198 respondents, 17 per cent
were people over the age of 35 who had choked or been choked before; 31 per cent
were people over 35 who had done neither; 32 per cent were people under 35 who had
choked or been choked before, and 20 per cent were people under 35 who had done
neither. Eat my shorts, YouGov.

choking became popular around six or seven years ago and are now a normal part of online life.

Which started first? Did young people start making memes about choking because they were choking each other? Did they see endless memes about choking during their formative sexual years so assumed it was a normal act? What's the chicken? What's the egg? Is it a vicious (or virtuous) cycle?

Even if the memes did influence our sexual practices, it would not be an entirely new phenomenon. As anyone who grew up with *Cosmopolitan* will tell you, sexual acts or positions have always gone in and out (hehe) of fashion. Still, choking is arguably a special case because it can be a dangerous act. If you don't know what you're doing or you're intoxicated while doing it, it can cause permanent physical damage, even death. The gendered nature of it is also concerning; in mainstream heterosexual culture, men tend to choke and women tend to get choked.

We still live in a world where women get beaten, raped and killed by men – can what is essentially a violent act done to women by men ever be entirely harmless? On the other hand, must we judge what people enjoy doing consensually in the sanctity of their own bedrooms? Can we not trust adult women to make choices that are right for them? But are personal choices ever made in a societal vacuum? Should we really pretend that women who grew up in an environment where violence against women is often glamorised are taking decisions entirely of their own volition? Can that line of thinking ever be productive if we are all ultimately the product of our environments? Even if a sex act becomes mainstream because of internet culture, does it change its very nature?

I ask these questions as someone who does not have any real answers to offer, despite having thought about them a lot. What I worry about is just how normal choking seems to me and how odd it has felt to be writing this when it is an act that should be treated as potentially dangerous.

As a largely horrifying study from the Indiana University School of Public Health pointed out in 2019, '[7 per cent of women] described feeling scared because their partner had tried to choke them unexpectedly' and '13 percent of sexually active girls ages 14 to 17 have already been choked'.

What happens when porn moves on to a new trend? What if that trend is even riskier? What happens to these women who are not into it but do so because they have no choice, or they were never taught to say no to their male partner?

I was lucky to be online when I was because I read the sex blogs of horny misfits and it taught me a lot without making me feel like I ever had to try any of it. I can yawn at the mention of spiked spanking paddles without having ever been near one myself. I'm comfortable with what I like and dislike doing because that is what my internet told me was okay.

Sure, I did also grow up watching naked women being poorly treated by naked men, but none of that ever felt real. I grew up watching Harry Potter but never believed I would grow up to be riding a broom – pun intended, thank you very much. Then again, I also benefited from having a mother who never shied away from difficult conversations and so I learned the basics from a reputable source at an appropriate age.

Not everyone did; I still remember being in biology class at around 12 and being asked to draw a naked man and a naked woman so the teacher could get a sense of how knowledgeable we were. One of the boys handed in a little drawing of a woman, entirely nude and held in handcuffs above her head.

What happened to that boy once he got to see real, naked women? I've definitely slept with some men like him, who felt like they wanted to have sex with the idea of women they had seen on their screen, and it wasn't particularly fun. It is a shame because there was a world in which the internet could have taught us all how to have better sex. It could have made it seem like a normal thing; something most of us do. It could have taught queer kids that it's fine to want to have queer sex and it could have shown them how to do it best.

It could have shown cis women how to get off in a way mainstream culture never did and it could have given tips to trans women about how to get used to their changing bodies. More generally, it could have taught us all that sex is really fun and nothing to be ashamed of, and that it is entirely fine to want to have tons of it, or none of it at all. Instead, it has been pushed to the margins yet again. The people in the boardrooms of PayPal and MasterCard and whoever else did not want to have to deal with naked and sticky people and so they shut it all down. The people in the boardrooms of Facebook and Tumblr wanted to be respectable and family friendly and able to work with squeaky clean brands so they banned flesh and fluids and that was the end of that.

This doesn't mean that sex has disappeared from the internet; it remains everywhere. According to a study on internet usage in the US conducted in 2021 by Statista, porn represents 13 and 20 per cent of web and mobile searches respectively. There are hundreds of thousands of naked people online and hundreds of millions of people willing to watch them. Sex has remained sort of hidden and quite wrong; something we know we are all at least a little bit obsessed with, but we like to keep a secret. The way we like to have sex with others is very obviously inspired by the sex we see online but we do not fully admit it. Sex is banned from all the mainstream platforms but we all choke each other now and that cannot have come out of nowhere.

The sex blogs have, for the most part, disappeared. I can no longer read about the weird and slightly gross things horny strangers get up to and it's disappointing. I had such high hopes for sex and the internet and – I'm sorry, I promise I didn't mean for this to be another dick joke – they fell flat. I have a hard time listening to the older and less online talking about it as a topic because deep down, I know that they're right: the internet has, all things considered, been bad for sex.

It has been positive in some ways, perhaps, but it isn't clear that it has made our relationship with sex that much healthier. Men still hurt women and women still feel they need to act and look a certain way to be fuckable, and of course it is vital that they are deemed fuckable. It's especially painful because I had a lovely time being young and curious online and it's sad that my experience is not – could not – be scalable. Well, there was the eye socket of that rotting sheep's skull, which I can still see at the back of my eyelids if I focus hard enough, but that was an acceptable trade-off. Nothing can ever be truly perfect.

All in all, it's also one of the few topics I feel

somewhat optimistic about; there will always be horny people out there and they will always find new and innovative ways in which to be horny. I believe that one day they will rise up and prove to everyone that the internet can be a force for lustful good, hopefully changing society at large in the process.

3

WHERE ARE WE?

Lost in Translation

Tell you what has been a weird thing to get used to: writing a book about the internet in the way one would write a book and not in a way one would write online. I've been using all these capital letters and these full stops and only ever one exclamation mark at a time – and there hasn't been a single stray line break.

I've tried to use words that everyone understands and referenced as few memes and tweets as possible, and when I have used them, I've made sure to explain what I meant by them. They were not a part of my speech but instead were examples that were not part of the prose. I wonder if it's made my writing less sincere, or at least different.

I've been writing about the internet like I write about politics or current affairs. It has been an interesting exercise. When my first book came out, my friends told me that they read it in my voice; the ones who listened to the audiobook said it was odd to hear words that were so clearly mine being spoken by someone else. I think it's because I have done most of my writing online; doing so fundamentally changes the way you engage with the written word. One Tumblr user, called Feynites, explained it well on their blog a few years ago:

> 'I actually thought for a long time that texting just made my mother cranky. But then I watched my sister send her a funny text, and my mother was laughing her ass off. But her actual texted response?
>
> "Ha... right."
>
> Like, she had actual goddamn tears in her eyes and that was what she considered an appropriate reply to the joke. I just marvelled for a minute, like "what the actual hell?" Texting and text-based chatting are, relatively, still pretty new and my mother's generation by and large didn't grow up writing things down in real-time conversations, they explained.
>
> So whereas people around my age or younger

tend to text like we're scripting our own dialogue and need to convey the right intonations, my mom writes her texts like she's expecting her Eighth grade English teacher to come and mark them in red pen. When she considers putting effort into how she's writing, it's always the lines of making it more formal or technically correct, and not along the lines of "how would this sound if you said it out loud?'"

I believe this cleavage began with MSN Messenger. Though people wrote in a more familiar fashion on blogs and forums than they did, say, at school or work, the immediacy of MSN was the game changer. Emails and posts could still read like letters to friends, as they were self-contained and, even if part of a wider conversation, did not assume that someone was reading as we posted.

Once we became able to talk to people we knew were actively in front of their screen as we were in front of ours, everything changed. We were talking to each other; it just so happened that we were using our fingers instead of our mouths.

(I'm very sorry, I'm going to have to pause for a moment to childishly laugh at the sentence 'we were using our fingers instead of our mouths.')

(Okay, I'm good.)

It entirely changed the way we communicated with one another online. After all, talking to someone face-to-face involves so much more than words; there is body language, eye contact, facial expression, tone, pace and everything else. A single sentence can have a thousand meanings depending on how it is said.

The classic example is 'She said she did not take his money'; depending on which word you decide to put the emphasis on, it can have eight different meanings. 'She *said* she did not take his money' gets a point across that is very different from 'She said she did not take *his* money', and so on. Similarly, something as innocuous as 'No, I'm not going to his party tonight' can have a myriad of meanings, depending on how you say it and what you look like while you're saying it. Are you sad that you can't make it to his party? Are you happy about it? Are you incensed that someone would even dare ask whether you'd be going to his party, given what happened between the two of you? Are you petulantly pointing out that you wouldn't be seen dead at a party as lame as his? The nuances are endless – traditional written speech cannot contain them all.

The problem was spotted quite early on among pioneers of the proto-internet. According to a piece published by *TIME* magazine in 2014, it is what led to the invention of the emoticon:

'Scott Fahlman, a computer scientist at Carnegie Mellon, noticed that conversations were going awry on electronic message boards the staff was using to communicate in the early 1980s. Jokes were being lost, tones were being misconstrued and unnecessary tirades were eclipsing the intended discussions. So Fahlman, then in his early 30s, made a simple, legendary suggestion: if you're being humorous or ironic, label your comment with a smiley face made of a colon, dash and parenthesis.'

By the time legions of teenagers joined MSN Messenger, emoticons had expanded and evolved; you could :) or :(but you could also :s and :/. Some people preferred to :-) but they were the odd ones; overall, we tended to :D and, ;) and, when being especially cheeky, :p.

Still, emoticons are probably the least interesting part of online written speech, since they are merely an add-on. Acronyms also aren't an intrinsic part of speech but deserve to be mentioned. For example, it's hard not to feel nostalgic about AFK, G2G and BRB – 'away from keyboard', 'got to go' and 'be right back'.

They were useful because we were not so wedded to our screens as we are now. Perhaps a computer had several users fighting over access; perhaps our mum had called us for dinner; perhaps we were going because we simply had something to go and do. Apart from flights, movies at the cinema and particularly tense meetings, when was the last time any of us just went offline for a while? Others like JK, ROFL, LOL and LMAO were closer in purpose to emoticons; by adding one of them to the end of a sentence, the user could make it clear that they were joking, or at the very least not being entirely serious.

Emoticons and acronyms are all fairly straight-forward because what they mean is obvious: a sad face means that someone is sad, 'just kidding' means that the person was not being serious, et cetera. Not every aspect of online language is as obvious. For example, I absolutely know that there is a difference between someone ending a sentence like..........this and someone ending a sentence like,,,,,,,,,,this, but I'm not sure I could explain it to you.

I have also been known to write down words ~like this~, which is obviously miles away from writing down words like *this* or like THIS, but I would beg you not to ask me what I meant by that. Similarly, '?', '???' and '? ? ?' are entirely distinct and so are 'hah', 'haha' and 'hahahaha', but how to put it in words?

It would be like trying to explain the specific meaning of facial expressions; if I'm in front of someone, I can tell you that they seem broadly happy or sad, and sound sarcastic or forlorn, but it would be tough to show my workings. Is it something in their eyes? The way their eyebrow moved? The blink-and-you-miss it smirk that appeared in one corner of their mouth?

It also doesn't help that none of these quirks and phrases are set in stone. In the days of MSN Messenger, overexcited teenagers would send messages overladen with exclamation marks. It didn't matter if the matter at hand wasn't especially exciting; if it was worth typing at all, it was worth ending like this!!!!!!! At some point this changed, and exclamation marks became altogether quite passé.

We were all cool and chilled out and the mere idea of excitement was simply quite gauche. I remember those years because I remember looking down on people who had clearly not got the memo and kept using exclamation marks. Were they unaware of how lame they seemed? Of course, I ended up being hoisted by my own petard in the late 2010s when exclamation marks became acceptable (and indeed encouraged) again.

At time of writing, I remain a !!!! enthusiast, going as far as beginning work messages with a jaunty 'hello!!', something which would have made my skin crawl only a few years ago. Will I still be doing this by the time this book comes out? There is no way of knowing – the ebbs and flows of online syntax are impossible to predict. Like real-life trends, they also tend to happen by osmosis. There are no online linguists who descend from the heavens every six months or so to tell us how to express ourselves.

In that respect, online lingo isn't dissimilar from other languages. As all polyglots will tell you, the best way to learn a new language is to go to a country where people speak it then let your brain do the rest. It's hard at first then it becomes second nature. In my experience of learning English, you know you've hit the jackpot once you find it hard to translate a word back into your own language, despite having used that word before.

Mine was 'awkward'; it became part of my everyday vocabulary but, when a French friend asked me what it meant, I couldn't really tell her. There isn't a French word that means 'awkward', not really; still, I had got enough of a sense of its meaning to use it correctly. An online equivalent could be 'smol', which I mentioned in a piece I wrote some years ago and will shamelessly bring back here, because it is very neat.

'According to Know Your Meme, it started in 2015 when young fans of a musician called Tyler Josephs took to calling him "smol bean", a cutesy but not entirely weird nickname. "Smol" then became an adjective used to mostly describe small and fluffy animals, which led to it getting its own meaning.

" ...at this point, smol isn't even a 'mispelling' of small anymore; it has its own connotations," explained 29-year old Teagan on their Tumblr. "While small is a regular adjective, smol acts more like a diminutive marker, which English has been lacking. In essence, a smol dog will always be a small dog, but not all small dogs are smol.'"

I remember researching this story and being very pleased I'd stumbled upon this explanation, as it'd put into words something I'd known but couldn't have adequately summed up myself. I could see something or someone and think of them as 'smol', but needed a third party to tell me what I meant by that.

Of course, 'smol' is easy because it's uncontroversial; cute boys don't tend to object to being called smol and fluffy puppies are rarely given a right of reply. Things tend to get dicier when the same dynamics are applied to other, more concrete issues. Words are important and the way we use them matters, but things can move so fast online that it's easy to get lost. In that respect, it is not unlike a high school; a slang term can be edgy, become widely popular, then be discarded in the space of about a month. It's hard to follow. Because I effectively live online, I usually pride myself on being able to track the various linguistic trends that come and go, but I do remember one that baffled me.

Though I'd spent many happy years on Tumblr by that point, the discovery of a trans acquaintance's blog in 2012 meant that I suddenly fell into a queerer side of the site, largely populated by trans kids and their fellow travellers. As I remember it, this is what happened:

- At first, trans people used the word 'trans' to describe themselves and others like them;
- Suddenly, some trans people on my Tumblr dashboard started calling themselves 'trans*';
- Suddenly, every trans person on my Tumblr dashboard called themselves 'trans*' and repudiated the use of 'trans' without the asterisk;
- Eventually, some trans people on my Tumblr dashboard started questioning the use of 'trans*';
- Eventually, every trans person on my Tumblr dashboard called out the use of 'trans*';
- In the end, everyone went back to using the word 'trans' to describe themselves and others like them.

Rationally, I know that it didn't happen in the course of about three weeks; still, this is how it felt. Being cisgender myself, I had no skin in the game; still, I had trans friends I didn't wish to offend and so followed the controversy with bated breath. I didn't want to be a bad ally but this rollercoaster of words that were bad then good then bad again felt stressful.

Having googled it since, it appears that the whole trans/trans* debate lasted for around two years, which is longer than my recollection but still stunningly short. Trans author Julie Serano wrote about it in 2015, at a point when trans had largely won over trans*, and called the incident a classic incident of 'word-sabotage'. It is not unique to the trans issue; having experienced it as a bisexual woman, I can explain how that process works.

Step 1: People call themselves bisexual, to denote their attraction to men, women and whoever else may be free and willing on a Saturday night.

Step 2: Instead of widening the definition of 'bisexual' to include attraction to non-binary people, some bisexual people start to call themselves pansexual instead, to denote the fact that they are not merely attracted to men and women, but to people of all genders and none.

Step 3: Because both pansexual and bisexual are now in use, it becomes assumed that people who willingly call themselves bisexual do not recognise the existence of non-binary people, or at least are implying that they are not attracted to them.

Step 4: 'Bisexual' becomes an exclusionary term.

Step 5: Just about enough people go 'hang on, what?' and the whole sorry mess is largely forgotten.

This is what happened with trans*. As Serano wrote, 'The way it was told to me, the asterisk is intended to serve the same "wild card" function that it does in search engines—thus, trans* would include trans, transgender, transsexual, transvestite, and so on.

'While I have no problems with the term trans*, I did dislike some of the dynamics that accompanied it during its rise in popularity. [...] Because many people viewed the asterisk as imparting broad inclusion, suddenly the use of the terms transgender and trans sans asterisk—which I have used in a broad inclusive manner for well over a decade—would sometimes be questioned, or might be interpreted as promoting exclusion. It is rather surreal to have the language you have long used as part of your activism shift in meaning or connotation so quickly.'

What is especially fascinating here is that trans* wasn't even new. The asterisk has come and gone from the word trans for a long time; the new generation of trans people and their allies – myself included – just had no idea about it. In a public Facebook post, trans woman Tobi Hill-Meyer explained: 'The first people I knew using it were all trans women computer science nerds that took it from the search function wild card (searching for car* would return results for "car" "carry" "card" and anything else starting with car).

'It was a way to shortcut the transgender vs trans-sexual infighting that was raging that whole decade and was a way to make a political statement that the distinction between transgender and transsexual was unimportant. It was originally an attempt to create space that included transgender women and transsexual women together.'

Fast forward to 2014 and, according to a poster made by LGBTQ educator Sam Killermann, trans* meant transgender/transsexual/transvestite/genderqueer/ genderfluid/non-binary/gender-fuck/genderless/ agender/non-gendered/third gender/two-spirit/bigender/ trans man/trans woman. The term was seamlessly brought back into use but the context had changed.

Trans* was originally used to bring two warring factions together for the greater good. Once queer identities and the online discourse around them became more complex and fragmented, its use became fraught. Because the internet facilitated immediate and horizontal debate, the entire thing also happened at breakneck speed. It was trans then it was trans* then it was trans again; had you chosen to be largely offline for about 18 months, you would have missed it all.

Still, it was fascinating – if puzzling – to follow as a bystander because the arguments came from all sides and they all had the same weight. The flatness of online meant that everyone with an opinion could get involved, which is why it got so messy. At least, the vast majority of cis people stayed out of it, as it had nothing to do with us, which was refreshing.

How much messier could it have been if everyone else had decided to join in?

This question is only slightly rhetorical, because we know just how messy it could have got if everyone had decided to join in. It did not happen with trans*, but it did with Karen a few years later. In fact, the Karen debate got so strained that typing the word just now made my shoulders tense, but it is regrettably worth exploring.

To the best of anyone's knowledge, Karen's life began on Black Twitter. There is no specific tweet or conversation to point to, but it is where she was born. Karen wasn't really special at the start. Before her there had been Becky – who came in standard format, 'with the good hair', or as a Barbecue edition – Cornerstore Caroline, Permit Patty and many more.

What these nicknames had in common was that they were used, mostly by American Black women, to describe types of unreasonable and usually racist American white women. Sometimes they call the police on a perfectly innocent cook-out; sometimes they call the police on a child selling water on a little street stall.

According to a *Guardian* piece from 2020, the Caroline, Becky, Patty or [insert your own alliteration here] is a 'white woman surveilling and patrolling Black people in public spaces and then calling the police on them for random, non-illegal infractions'.

A Karen started out as much the same, but the term exploded thanks to one Amy Cooper, a 40-year-old white investment manager who went out to walk her dog in Central Park one afternoon. She stumbled upon Christian Cooper, a 57-year-old Black birdwatcher, who asked her to put her dog on a leash; she refused, despite being in a part of the park where leashing was required.

He insisted, then she called the police on him. 'I'm calling the cops ... I'm gonna tell them there's an African-American man threatening my life,' she told him angrily while he filmed her. What happened next is what sealed her fate; though she had been seething, her tone changed once she started talking to the 911 operator.

Suddenly sounding distressed and terrified, she

talked of being threatened by 'an African-American man'. Though she did end up putting her dog back on a leash in the end, the damage was done. The video was posted online, it went viral and both she and the concept of 'Karen' went viral.

'It was through that performance that Amy Cooper took on the mantle of an American archetype: the white woman who weaponizes her vulnerability to exact violence upon a Black man,' that same *Guardian* piece explained. 'In history, she is Carolyn Bryant, the adult white woman whose complaint about a 14-year-old Emmett Till led to his torture and murder at the hands of racist white adults. In literature, she is Scarlett O'Hara sending her husband out to join a KKK lynching party or Mayella Ewell testifying under oath that a Black man who had helped her had raped her. In 2020, she is simply Karen.'

The term was neat because it managed to whittle down a complex and historically significant phenomenon into one single name. If you were to describe someone as a Karen, people would know exactly what you meant – or would they?

While this conversation was happening on Black Twitter, the rise of Karen was also taking place in a very different corner of the internet. In December 2017, the subreddit forum r/FuckYouKaren was launched by Karmacop97, a kid from California. The page was inspired by a fellow Redditor named Fuck_You_Karen, who became known for his incendiary posts about his ex-wife. You can guess what her name was.

Though the subreddit was originally, according to a *Vox* piece, created to 'compile the lore behind this guy's relationship,' according to a *Vox* piece, it soon became a place where people could 'call out all kinds of "Karen"-ish behavior'.

'A Karen divorces her husband and takes the kids, is a pseudoscientist/anti-vaxxer/flat-earther, an MLM participant, an avid user of Facebook to post shitty motivational posts/'Live Laugh Love,' and more,' karmacop97 told *Vox*. 'Our Karen in the wild won't satisfy all of [these attributes], but she can still be a true Karen.'

It also goes without saying that, as with many things on *Reddit* and memes about 'the ex-wife who took the kids', this iteration of Karen was largely used by men and frequently was misogynistic. In this context, a Karen was a woman who was likely to be white, middle-aged, too assertive for her own good, yet too twee to be taken seriously.

Because our two Karens rose to prominence at around the same time, it soon became hard to differentiate between the Karen who was 'a critique of entitled white womanhood' (as per a headline from Bitch Media) and the Karen who 'turned the weans against us' (my paraphrasing). It did not help that they shared some of the same characteristics: all Karens tended to be white, straight, middle class or above, in their thirties or above, and too mouthy for their own good.

That last one was a problem; while some Karens used their status to harass Black people and other marginalised communities, other Karens had merely committed the crime of being a woman with a personality. Similarly, a 'can I speak to the manager?' attitude can be used for good or evil, but because of the inherent duality of Karen, it became hard to tell which was which.

This all came to a head in 2020 when everyone started calling everyone else Karen and no one quite knew what anyone meant by that. On one side, some white feminists argued that the term was inherently sexist; on the other, progressive activists and people of colour argued that it was about a necessary tool to discuss racial dynamics. Neither was completely wrong; neither was completely right.

In truth, the meaning of Karen changed depending on who used it – men or women, white or Black – which was an issue because on the internet, nobody knows you're a dog. If someone posted a tweet complaining about a Karen online, it was often impossible to tell which angle they were coming from. Were we meant to applaud or admonish them?

Posts could also easily switch from one category to the other because it is easy to lose all context online, especially if something is screengrabbed, goes viral or both. Black Twitter lost the vocabulary it had created for itself and sexists everywhere got to merrily mock women they felt wronged by.

As with trans and trans*, this all happened incredibly quickly; though language has been evolving ever since people started speaking, words now come in and out of fashion faster than ever. It matters because the words we use make us who we are. Real life has accents and local slang and the internet has memes, phrases and lingo laden with communal meaning. All we have to define ourselves is what we type, but because we have all been gradually squashed into the same spaces, words can easily slip from one group to another, losing their spark and significance in the process.

It is a crime with real victims but few conscious perpetrators, which makes things quite complex. Because we are not all talking face to face and no one is expected to google every new phrase they come across, words that are attached to certain communities can be taken away from them more or less by accident.

This especially tends to happen with African-American Vernacular English; from lit and woke to bae and salty, AAVE has become culturally dominant online. All words do not follow the same path, but many of them tend to travel from Black online circles to LGBT ones, then onto straight white women and to everyone else.

The missing link here is drag culture, which was long dominated by Black and Latina queens in the US, and which comes with its own vocabulary. As a piece in *Wired* from 2018 explained, 'If you're new to drag culture, watching *Drag Race* [...] can feel a little like stepping into unknown linguistic territory. In watching queens serve any and all manner of realness, viewers are absorbing an argot that has birthed everything from "realness" to "kiki" to "spilling the tea." And unless you've been living off the grid for the past few years, you've likely been "yas, queen!"-ed into oblivion.'

In a way it is spreading the joy; drag is a fun, provoking and radical art form, and the more that partake in it, the merrier. On the other hand, many of the words that are now mainstream belonged to marginalised communities, who had to create their own families and forms of entertainment because no one else would have them. The language they developed is more than just words; it is a world onto itself.

In this context, 'yas' now being described by Urban Dictionary as 'An annoying expression used by girls expressing extreme liking' is disheartening. Similarly, 'woke' was never meant to become an insult levelled at progressives by middle-aged newspaper columnists, but you cannot squeeze toothpaste back into the tube. Once words escape, they are lost. If how we speak is who we are, what does that mean for people's sense of identity?

It is also worryingly easy for the opposite to happen and for malevolent groups to make mundane phrases and memes their own, destroying them in the process. I still mourn the loss of Pepe, the horrible little frog that became popular online in early 2015. I already hated it at the time, but I was seeing a man I really liked and he enjoyed annoying me by sending me various versions of the meme – the worse, the better.

Our conversations online mainly consisted of a back and forth of Pepe memes; rare ones, upsetting ones, ones we'd found in increasingly niche corners of the internet. He was as online as I was and it was our way of getting closer to each other. Our time together ended abruptly after a few months, but somehow Pepe kept a special place in my heart. I had never dated someone who was quite as online as I was – and have not since then – and it was a nice, if odd memory of our time together.

It was also short-lived, because Pepe was claimed by white supremacists and the alt-right just a few months later, at the start of the 2016 US election campaign. People – men, mostly – who were just as online as he and I had been had decided to use it for evil, specifically because it had appealed to 'normies'. If you show that horrible little frog to someone now, they will almost certainly think of Trump-supporting trolls.

What this means in practice is that I no longer get to enjoy Pepe, because it is no longer mine. I loathed that little frog at the beginning but I had grown fond of it; the memory is now irrevocably stained and there is nothing I can do about it. This is the internet and nothing is ours; we base our conversations, identities and relationships around shared words and memes, but it can all get away from us at a moment's notice.

✳ ✳ ✳

As a side note and a prelude to what is to come – writing about Pepe pushed me to look at past Gmail chat conversations I had with the man I was seeing in 2015. Because our time together ended poorly, I have not read them since, but I have occasionally clicked on the tab just to remind myself that it is there. I would see his last message to me, which was about nothing in particular, and I would not have the heart to scroll up.

I went to look at it today and thought that I would scroll up this time, at least a bit. I clicked and the conversation was gone; maybe he has deleted it, maybe he no longer has that email address. I dislike him too much ever to ask him. Still, it has made me sad; I feel robbed of memories I assumed I would always be able to access. I feel betrayed because I had no say in it.

How can the internet feel so small and personal when deep down, it is so obviously boundless, cold and uncaring? One moment, it feels like we were handed all the power in the world; another, it becomes clear that none of this ever truly belonged to us.

✱ ✱ ✱

To return briefly to Feynites' well-meaning mother, it feels worth mentioning that many people online do not think about what they type at all. I know this because I am friends with some of them. Sometimes I am sent memes and emojis so old they are nearly vintage and it puzzles me. It then makes me wonder if they have an easier life; if they are the ones living as adults and I am the one still stuck in a virtual high school, anxious to only use the cool words that the cool kids like.

I have been in full-time employment for nine years and I still bristle whenever someone sends me a short message with a full stop at the end. I am always convinced that they are angry at me; I can rationally think that it is simply that they did not grow up online, but I cannot shake the feeling of panic. There are people who now spend every day online because that is the done thing but they only see it as an extension of real life.

In real life there are full stops at the end of sentences, why wouldn't there be on the internet? This is why it is hard to write about online language; not because I am not writing in the way I usually write online, but because talking about online language means talking about everything else. I have explained some things and shared some anecdotes and used some examples but it was always going to only skirt around the edges of the issue.

Every single one of these chapters is, in a way, about the way we talk to each other online. Isn't it all we do, all day long? It was silly of me to think that I could round it all up in a few thousand words – however they may be written.

Friend or Foe?

Thinking about the way we use words on and around the internet made me think about the way in which I think about the algorithm. The algorithm is always singular, as far as I am concerned. I am aware it is technically not a single "it" but instead a mechanism used differently by each separate website or company, but deep down, I know it is always one and the same.

The algorithm wasn't always there; for many years I was in charge of my own actions on the internet. I visited pages and blogs because I had stumbled upon them once and enjoyed returning to them, like a city or a bar. Sometimes I was wandering, sometimes I was lost. I cannot remember when the algorithm arrived in my life because its presence was only small at first, barely noticeable. I went on my online journeys and it sat in the corner of the screen, sometimes, pushing me down new alleyways and towards old haunts.

At first the ads it gave me were adjacent to my actual desires, in the way that presents early on in relationships that never quite hit the mark. I didn't really care for them, or about them. Eventually the algorithm got better; it found out more about me and we became closer.

I remember clicking on an Instagram ad once, in 2018, and being astounded by it; I had never been correctly advertised to online and for some reason I had been proud of it. I could spend my days in front of a screen but I was too complex for the screen to capture my real essence.

I bought a bra from the brand Instagram had given me and since then I have bought several more bras from that brand. I have even recommended it to some friends of mine, each time feeling like a little cog in a machine I do not like. The algorithm knows me well now; I click on ads and suggested pages and accounts often, especially on Instagram but occasionally elsewhere.

I resisted it for years because I wanted my travels across the internet to be my own, but it was futile. The algorithm and I spent a lot of time together and it was bound to get to know me better. At some point our relationship became more reciprocal; having let my guard down, I decided to embrace it.

I listen to a lot of music on Spotify which, for the past few years, has meant that I listen to a lot of my Daily Mixes on Spotify. The algorithm makes them for me; it looks at what I have been listening to then sorts the songs into six different playlists, arranged by era and genre. Sometimes it only gives me the classics it knows I like; often, it adds on a few other songs I have never listened to, in the hope that I will like them too.

When I discover a new band or artist that I enjoy, I now make sure to listen to their songs on loop for a few days, not because I want to but so I can bring them to the algorithm's attention. Like a woman in a nineties movie leaving shop catalogues open on a specific page in the months before Christmas, I hint that it is what I would like to get more of. Eventually the algorithm will realise what I am trying to do and it will add the songs onto the relevant Daily Mix, like an occasionally forgetful but ultimately caring spouse. I didn't want it to be in my life but now it is here so I may as well make my peace with it.

It is an odd relationship and one I now feel, despite my best efforts, quite attached to; a friendship I did not want in my life but which forced its way in anyway. When the algorithm recommends me something I do not like, it feels like a betrayal. We have spent so much time together! Were you not paying attention? Did you not care? Do you even have any interest in me? I mean, bath salts, for heaven's sake! Have I ever mentioned even a passing interest in them to you? Who do you think I am? And so on.

It reminds me of the story of the roomba, which has made the rounds on Tumblr and elsewhere so many times that I could nearly type it up by heart. It was this:

'*voidspacer:*

My roomba is scared of thunderstorms

I was sitting at my desk just a few minutes ago, drawing, and a really loud crack of thunder went off – no power surges or anything, just thunder – and my roomba fled from its dock and started spinning in circles

I currently now have an active roomba sitting quietly on my lap

systlin:

Humans will pack bond with *anything.*'

Much as I want to make fun of the person petting the worried roomba, at least they are petting a physical object with a straightforward purpose. I have, as far as I can tell, managed to pack bond with – well, I was going to google 'algorithm' to find out how they are made but I have realised I do not want to.

I have managed to pack bond with an algorithm, which is always singular because it follows me around the internet and I will not hear anything to the contrary. I am intellectually aware of the fact that there are people in Silicon Valley or heaven knows where else who want to control my movements so they can sell me things so that they can get rich, but it is all distant and irrelevant.

My algorithm is small and it is here with me; I arguably preferred my life online when I was alone and I could take all my decisions myself but I was not given a choice. I now have a companion with me on all my journeys and I take it personally when it does not pay the correct amount of attention to me, which is 'a lot'.

I know I have been talking about it like I think it is a person but I don't. The algorithm is a cat; I can tell because words matter and, when I think about the algorithm, I think of it like it is my cat. One day, it was outside my window then one day, some months after that, it was in my living room.

I didn't really want it to be there but the internet is my home and I cannot leave it just because there is now a cat inside of it. The internet is my home but it does not belong to me; I do not get to decide what happens inside of it and must simply get used to whoever I am finding myself sharing it with. It is the deal I made, a long time ago, without really realising that I was making it in the first place.

It works as a metaphor in my head because cats also adopt you more than you adopt them, and do not really give you a choice. Sometimes they are well-meaning but what they do is bring you a half-dead mouse as a gift, because they do not really understand what you want. The algorithm wasn't there and then it was there, and sometimes it thinks I want to buy Crocs. I will never want a half-dead mouse; I will never want to buy Crocs. Still, we both share this home now and well, I appreciate the effort.

Bubble, Burst

I have no idea what to do online anymore. It is something I had vaguely noticed before but it really became clear during the first lockdown of 2020. I would sit on my couch all day working on my laptop, then once I was done with work, I would sit on my couch all evening, looking at my laptop.

I wanted my leisure internet to be different from my work hours internet but it wasn't. Often, I would sit there, motionless, staring at a blank browser, and realise that there were no websites I wanted to visit. That is why I eventually got into video games; I was conditioned to want to spend most of my day in front of a screen, but the main screen at my disposal was no longer enough.

I remember a time when going online in the evening felt like a bus route. I had a strict schedule that I would stick to; a number of blogs I would check out in a specific order, hoping each time that it would have been updated that day. There were websites I liked as well, that I knew I could waste time on; if things really were desperate, I would go to *StumbleUpon* and let it guide me to random and miscellaneous corners of the internet.

Even as blogs started to disappear for good in the early 2010s, my daily routine was artificially propped up by places like *BuzzFeed*. It is both a website and a company I have come to loathe – for personal and professional reasons – but at the time I was merely thankful it allowed me to mindlessly pass the time.

As someone with an attention deficit disorder, I cannot bear to stay idle, or let myself feel bored for even one minute. It is why I partied a lot when I was younger; being head-splittingly hungover was the easiest way I found to slow down without exploding. The internet helped too because for a long time, it was impossible to be bored online. There were people to meet! Places to discover! Secrets to unearth! Trivial facts to learn! It was exhilarating. I did not notice it changing because it was slow and gradual; Facebook was fascinating for a long time and so were Twitter, Instagram and all the others. They remained new and shiny for longer than they should have and we were so taken in by them that we failed to notice that everything around them was collapsing.

The epiphany came eventually, but by then it was too late; over half the people I interviewed for this book said they missed blogs terribly, but none of them have one still. The only thing we do on the internet now is scroll – we scroll down to look at tweets, pictures, memes and jokes because they are all in the same place and so are we.

Things are, for the most part, either entirely public or entirely private; the spaces that were technically open but quite hard to find no longer exist. It is one of the worst things that has happened to me and I hate that I was one of the people who made it happen. Had we not thoughtlessly flocked to these gigantic platforms, they never would have become gigantic in the first place. If only we'd known what we were doing.

✳✳✳

If you have even a passing interest in current affairs and what happens online, you will have heard this theory at some point in the past few years: society is collapsing and it is because we all live in echo chambers. The internet, the theory goes, allows us to surround ourselves with people who look like us, sound like us and, perhaps more importantly, have all the same opinions as us.

It is why countries like the US and Britain are so divided and why we now scream past each other instead of trying to find common ground. Echo chambers are dangerous for democracy because people are at their best when they are frequently confronted with people and views they disagree with. Because we now get to cherry-pick our social networks, we are all living in our own little burrows, unaware of what our fellow citizens think and say.

It is a popular theory and one that has been around for several years. 'Echo Chambers Are Dangerous – We Must Try To Break Free Of Our Online Bubbles' is a piece the *Guardian* published in 2017; 'How To Break Out Of Your Social Media Echo Chamber' is a guide *WIRED* helpfully published in 2020.

I have another theory: all of this is profoundly wrong and misunderstands how the internet has changed over the past decade or so. There is a fundamental problem with how we live our lives online and it is that we are now all together, all of the time. The spaces in which I talk to my family are the same spaces in which I talk to my friends and interact with my work contacts. My father follows me on Twitter and so do my childhood friends and several government ministers. We have all been squished into the same dashboards, timelines and feeds, and we have no idea how to deal with it.

We are, after all, not meant to be the exact same person to everyone we encounter, not because people are inherently duplicitous but because that is how we function. You will not make the same jokes to your aunt, a school friend or your partner, just like you would not wear flip-flops to the office even if you own a pair to go to the beach.

We are built to be multifaceted because we are social beings; at no point in their history did humans roam alone. For a community to work as it is intended to, everyone involved in it needs to tweak their behaviour, consciously or unconsciously. There is a reason why people who pride themselves on always being honest, no matter how coarse their truth is, are not especially prized as friends. If you are not taking the feelings of the person in front of you into account when talking to them, it is a soliloquy and not a conversation.

This dynamic applies to public speaking as well. Were I to give a speech at a wedding, I would rather be briefed beforehand about who the guests at the wedding will be. Knob gags are fine in front of certain audiences, but frowned upon in front of others. The problem with the internet is that we are either giving the best man speech in front of every single person we know, or in front of a crowd hiding in darkness.

Let's take the former first, which largely applies to Facebook – as it happens, I have a useful anecdote that illustrates the problem well. In 2012, a rumour spread wildly that Facebook had suffered a widescale bug, which had put all private messages sent between 2007 and 2009 on users' walls for all to see. I wish I could say I didn't fall for it and merely smirked as people around me panicked. This would be a lie. A friend forwarded me the message at the time, I checked my own wall and the walls of my friends and nearly had a heart attack.

There were posts about nights out and the boys we'd gone home with; posts about drugs and posts sharing gossip about people we named. I frantically deleted everything from my wall then spent some time trying to phrase desperate messages to people I hadn't spoken to in several years. A few hours later, *TechCrunch* published a story on the supposed bug, including this official comment by Facebook: 'Every report we've seen, we've gone back and checked. We haven't seen one report that's been confirmed [of a private message being exposed]. A lot of the confusion is because before 2009 there were no likes and no comments on wall posts. People went back and forth with wall posts instead of having a conversation [in the comments of single wall post.]'

The entire experience was gobsmacking. Had we really been sharing all this stuff in full view of everyone?

Yes, we had been; Facebook could not have been clearer. Of course, it was partly because the website's layout at the time did not allow us to do anything else, as the comment pointed out. Still, it felt more like a behavioural issue than a technological one; even if we were encouraged to post publicly, why did we do it?

It was shocking because by 2012, most of us had many friends on Facebook; we had relatives and loose acquaintances and all these people we'd picked up along the way, who were now part of our daily lives. What we shared then was different from what we shared in the late noughties, when Facebook largely was for friends and people whose names we'd scribbled on pieces of paper in clubs so we could add them once at home. I even remember being called Margaret S. on Facebook when I first joined in 2008, which is both a mundane fact and proof that it still hadn't fully grown into what it would become. Some time later, I resentfully changed it to Marie Le Conte because I realised that no one else was using their online nickname on it anymore. I was beginning to look a bit silly, like that one child still taking their beloved plushy to nursery.

By 2012, the internet had become a different place, both because more people had begun to use it frequently and because all those people were spending time in the same spaces. Though it was possible to have different Facebook accounts for different purposes – something

I tried out for a while – it was so discouraged by the platform itself that it never felt worth the effort. We all became the best man, giving a speech to everyone we have ever met and expected to entertain every single one of them. Is it really a surprise that Facebook eventually lost its shine? Still, giving a best man speech to everyone you have ever met is not quite as bad as giving a best man speech in front of an audience you cannot see. It may be tough to try and be both palatable and interesting to people who represent very different areas of your life, but it could be worse.

In my experience, things are even dicier when the audience is the mystery – precisely because, as discussed earlier, we cannot be ourselves if we do not know who we are engaging with. There is no constant version of you and there is no constant version of me: a person will have traits that they take into every social interaction but they cannot go through life acting exactly the same with everyone.

This creates friction online because we often do not know who we are addressing, especially on open platforms like Twitter. It is something that hit me like a brick in the summer of 2020; a few months previously, I'd decided to create a private account, to which I'd brought around 800 of my closest mutuals. My main account had about 75,000 followers and I had been tweeting all day every day for years, but the constant abuse and paranoia about potential future abuse had driven me to this smaller, locked account.

Before that, friends frequently asked how I handled sharing quite intimate details of my life with this many people, time after time. I generally shrugged and explained that I was used to it; the account had started small then grown and grown, and why should I change what I post if it is what people enjoy about me? I was a frog having a lovely time in an increasingly hot bath.

This stopped being the case when I started spending most of my time tweeting to 800 people instead. Whenever I went back to my main account, @youngvulgarian, my heart started beating faster. Suddenly, I had stage fright: 75,000 people! A number of people Wikipedia describes as a large town! What could I possibly want to share with the equivalent of the entire population of Harrogate? Suddenly, my friends' concerns made sense: how on earth had I been posting about my hangovers and half-formed thoughts on politics to such a huge crowd?

Though I am a bit of an extreme example, I do think that a lot of people on Twitter are their own version of the frog pleasantly swimming in not-quite-boiling water. We start tweeting – or posting on Instagram – at a point when we do not have many followers and our spaces feel quite intimate. Of course, they are technically public, but why would anyone care about what we are saying?

The audience that we create in our head is a small one, because assuming that anyone in the world who has access to the internet could potentially be reading what we are writing would be paralysing. No one writes with everyone in the world in mind; that is not how brains work, nor is it how the internet encourages us to think. This very specific dynamic, I believe, is the main reason why we often struggle to figure out how to be a semi-functioning society online.

I'll elaborate:

1. You can laugh about everything, but not with everyone …

… is a rough translation of a very famous quote by French comedian Pierre Desproges, which he followed up with 'It is better to laugh about Auschwitz with a Jew than to play Scrabble with Klaus Barbie'. Desproges died in 1988 so never got to see how well his words applied to the internet. You can laugh about everything as long as the audience is the right one and, though I would argue that some jokes are so offensive they are out of bounds no matter who you are telling them to, the vast majority of them aren't. Still, even if a joke is not objectively offensive, you may be better off not telling it to people who may find it distasteful.

The problem with, say, Twitter, is that you can have a set audience and feel you can safely make a joke about X, because the audience in question contains no Xs. If, however, your tweet becomes popular enough to get retweeted even a few times, it will get a bigger audience. With each new retweet, the likelihood that the tweet will eventually reach an X grows. When it does, it will feel like a personal attack to X, which is unreasonable because they were not part of the original audience, but also reasonable because it did end up on their timeline.

It is usually described as 'context collapse', but I prefer to call it the Opera Singer Conundrum. In 2017, I was living in a lovely ground-floor flat in south London; a few months after moving in, I realised that an opera singer lived upstairs and that she enjoyed practising her singing with the windows open. It was incredibly charming at first and made me feel like I was living in an arthouse movie. It got progressively less charming with time, as it is simply not pleasant to get woken up by opera singing every other morning.

I posted a tweet about it at some point and gave it no second thoughts. It did reasonably well and caused me no trouble – until, that is, it reached Opera Singer Twitter. Did you know there is a corner of Twitter in which professional opera singers congregate? I did not, but I soon suffered their wrath as they tripped over themselves to castigate me and defend my upstairs neighbour. One even suggested that I should be grateful for having daily access to something people usually pay a lot of money for.

It was funny and benign but I still think of it often, because it functioned in the same way as most bigger, more dramatic and more upsetting online wars. I posted something mocking opera singers because I considered them to be outsiders and assumed that they were outsiders to my followers as well. It was the online equivalent of being at a house party and lightly mocking some of the people in the living room while hiding out in the kitchen. When the post started getting retweeted, the dynamics changed on a very fundamental level; to the people in the living room, I had just walked in and mocked them to their faces. There are two versions of events and they are both correct.

It is something you see happen again and again online and is often frustrating because no one is ever completely wrong and no one is ever completely right. You cannot reasonably be expected to only post things that no one among the millions of Twitter users could ever find insulting, but if something does end up on the timeline of one of those millions of users, they have a right to react directly, even if it feels like overkill to the original poster.

2. Talking behind people's backs isn't just easy –
it's fun too!

Human societies are made of cleavages – people are
young and old, wealthy and poor, rural or metropolitan,
queer or straight, and so on. It is, for the most part,
easy to go through life without thinking about them too
much; we are all our own mishmash of identities and
it would be exhausting to always see others in direct
opposition to ourselves. Life is a rich tapestry, and so
forth. Still, a good and healthy way to share a society
with those who aren't exactly like us is to be able to
have at least some separate spaces.

As a woman, I enjoy occasionally complaining about
men with my female friends; though I get along well with
my more working-class friends, I am sure they like to air
their frustrations with middle-class people when I am
not around. Our lives are made of over-lapping circles,
but they do not overlap completely. Well, they didn't
use to; once everyone got online, it became worryingly
easy to eavesdrop on what others say about us.

Take generational wars, for example. They are
tedious and overdone but quite useful to consider in
this context. When did they start? It is hard to tell, but
the *Atlantic* did publish 'Boomers vs. Millennials: The
Fight of a Generation (or Two)' in late 2011, which tells
us that things were already starting to heat up then.

By 2018, the idea that millennials and boomers (born, respectively, between 1981 and 1996 or 1946 and 1964) loathed each other was so popular that clickbait factory *Bored Panda* could publish something like '81 Times Millennials Got So Tired Of Baby-Boomers They Just Had To Clapback'. In 2020, the *Observer* attempted to call for a truce, pleading: 'Boomers v Millennials: let's call off the hostilities'.

If the entire conflict managed to pass you by, the writer of that last piece put it quite neatly: 'In the blue corner, the OK Boomers with their final-salary pensions and mortgage-free homes; in the avocado-green corner, Millennials. Millennial beef with Boomers is clear: at its heart a sense that they selfishly squandered their position as the most privileged generation ever. The opposing view is often distilled down to a distaste for snowflakery, with a side order of entitlement.'

The entire thing bores me to death, but it is a frustratingly good example to use. Though some economic factors do mean that we millennials have it objectively less good than people of our parents' generation, I do not believe that is the sole reason behind our mutual animosity. Instead, we have been spending too much time in each other's company.

It is entirely normal for people who were born several decades apart to have different tastes, interests and beliefs, and even a different sense of humour.

Advertisers wouldn't think of us as distinct age groups before designing their campaigns otherwise. I do not watch the same TV shows as my grandmother and would be ready to bet that you do not dress exactly the same as someone 30 years older than you. My mother hates some of the clothes I wear and that is fine; if anything, it would be more worrying if we went to all the same shops.

The problem is that until the people who are my mum's age decided to get online, I spent relatively little time with them. I was broadly aware of their views but they were peripheral to me. Similarly, people born at around the same time as my father probably have a vague idea of what people in their twenties get up to, but little interest in finding out more – that is the way things should be. After all, what could be more normal than old people complaining about the ways of the youths and young people finding their elders dull and embarrassing? If there were no generational splits on tastes and beliefs, societies would never evolve and culture would stagnate. Though you could argue until recently that the bad blood between millennials and boomers was in some way unique, it is clearly no longer the case.

At some point in 2021, millennials realised they were no longer young. We had been sniping at people calling us annoying children for years, but we weren't serious, not really; secretly, I think we enjoyed being the main characters of the internet. The change was slow then happened all at once; suddenly, Gen Z took over and there was nothing we could do about it. Their fashion was everywhere and so were their memes, music tastes and aesthetics.

I hate most of it and it is quite liberating – finally, I understand how my parents felt when I dressed myself as a teenager. Why on earth would they want to wear what we wore 20 years ago? Can't they tell they look silly? Crucially, though, I wish I could be observing them from afar. I would love to lean into my newfound old age and harmlessly complain about today's youths in peace.

Instead, Gen Z are everywhere I look online and, perhaps more importantly, they are talking back. They do not like our skinny jeans and they do not like our side partings; the fact that we grew up with Harry Potter is mortifying to them, as are most things we do and say. This has caused some millennials online to hit back, which is perhaps the saddest thing of all: if teenagers cannot make fun of people in their thirties, what can they do? But then I am sure that at some point something will go viral and it will make me feel angry and defensive, because that is what happens when we all share the same spaces. The circles should overlap a bit but now they overlap completely. I look forward to

Gen Z ageing and joining us in the unhappy realisation that they are no longer the freshest blood around.

3. The reasonable function of transitional demands

Most forms of campaigning involve at least a little bit of lying. Some people may campaign for one very specific and straightforward change to society, in which case they probably do not have to lie, but everyone else has to be economical with the truth in order to get their way. Let's take immigration as an example. I personally believe that we should live in a world with little to no borders; it would be my ideal end goal.

I am aware that this is a fringe view, at least for now, and I know that if I and people like me were to argue for open borders today, people would laugh in our faces. Instead, what pro-immigration advocates must do first is to argue for an immigration system that is less cruel. We should take in a few more refugees and make it a bit easier to get citizenship; that is all we ask.

Well, it isn't, but the people we are making the argument to do not know that. If 20, 30 years down the line, we end up in a world where it is a fair bit easier to get citizenship and we take in quite a lot more refugees and people are broadly happy with it, then open borders may no longer look so fanciful as an idea. Still, if people were to say 'Oh! They want to open up our borders!' today we would deny it, of course, and it would not be entirely false. We do not want to open up our borders *today*. We are only lying a little bit – it is how campaigning works.

Still, there is a problem here and it is that campaigners do not solely need to talk to the rest of the population; they need to talk to each other as well, to decide what to do and how to do it. They must be able to gather and ask questions like: do we really want open borders? If so, when do we think they could be opened up? How could we argue for them when the time comes? How would these borders work once they are open? And so on. They need spaces in which they can be entirely honest about their aims.

What happens when both their conversations with the public and these internal conversations happen in the same spaces and in full view of everyone else? Culture wars happen. Different sides used to talk among themselves then meet in public forums to discuss polished and targeted versions of their views. Arguments now happen everywhere, all the time.

It is deeply unhelpful for two reasons. The first is that, as we've just discussed, messages need to be targeted to be efficient and most campaigners agree that change needs to be gradual. It is now extremely easy for, say, anti-immigration activists to find a Twitter conversation between immigration advocates discussing the feasibility of open borders and dramatically reveal it as the end goal. If you are someone who is open to a slight relaxing of immigration rules, this may well shift your views back to a more anti-immigration stance.

The second is that everyone is now, if they so wish, able to have a voice online, which is a good thing in some ways but a very bad one in others. It is undeniably positive that people from underrepresented backgrounds, for example, now get to participate in public discourse more than they otherwise would have. It is, however, considerably less than ideal that anyone with a political affiliation and a Twitter account can be treated as representative of an entire movement.

It is an issue that keeps cropping up in party politics. If, say, you're a Labour Party member and activist and someone who supports open borders, how should you behave online? If some bad faith actors pick up on your social media posts and say, 'Look! If you vote for the Labour Party, you're voting for guys who support open borders!' and that turns off voters, is that your fault?

Equally, if you have strongly-held beliefs and want to shift the internal debate in your party in the long run, why shouldn't you make your views known? And if you're not an elected official, should anyone be telling you what to do? It is something we saw happen a lot when Jeremy Corbyn was leader of the Labour Party. If

@DaddyTrotsky69 has 'Jeremy Corbyn supporter' in her bio and wants borders to open tomorrow, what would stop anti-Corbyn activists from saying, 'Be careful, this is what this guy's supporters want'?

It may not be fair, but politics rarely is, online or off-line. This dynamic has poisoned most online discourse on both political and social issues. In order to debate properly, we cannot be debating all the time, but if every side of every argument is online at the same time, it is impossible not to always feel like you're at war.

As my friend Io Dodds pointed out to me, it is, in practice, a structural issue: 'It's often the case that people inside one interest group only see the worst and most bizarre content and takes of the other group that will conflict most with them. That's the only time they're in contact with other groups, they see the worst stuff that's been held up for their ridicule and it's being pre contextualised for them as "this is going to be ridiculous, time to laugh and mock".'

The problem is that it then becomes harder for people to switch sides on an issue or simply float around without having really picked a side. If what you are being sold is the worst possible version of the side of an argument, it is likely that you will react strongly – and very negatively – to it. As a result, social media platforms tend to swallow vague moderates and centrists and spit out hardened radicals.

This proliferation of debate can also, perhaps counterintuitively, stifle genuine and productive conversations. Discussions are often at their most fruitful when they involve people who do not disagree completely with each other, but instead are broadly on the same side. By exploring nuances, people can often reach better and more thought-out positions, which benefits everyone in the long run.

For this to happen, however, the spaces must be seen as relatively safe. It is something I think about often in the context of gender issues; as someone who supports the rights of transgender people, there are things I wish I could say to people on my side, from arguments I believe should be retired to angles I think are better to highlight. I do not mention them on Twitter because I know that bad faith actors are likely to see those points and use them to their own advantage, which is the opposite of what I want. Instead, I usually stay quiet and let the debate get worse and worse. How many people are doing the same?

This is true of all issues, from party politics to specific topics like gender, race, sexism and whether *Marvel* movies are real cinema. We are not only always in conflict, but often at risk of fighting against people who have fringe views but are portrayed as representative of an entire movement. Our arguments are bad because there are no real spaces in which we can discuss them with people who agree with us. Our spaces make us feel tense because we never feel truly safe in them anymore. Our internet is both open and flat, and it is not a nice place to be in.

The Invisible Panopticon

There is someone I would like you to meet; she is called Jessica, she works in social media and she is in her early thirties. We met in unusual circumstances.

In November 2010, I lived in Shoreditch and I was not studying at UCL. I was seeing a man who was around my age and who was also not studying at UCL. The student protests against rising university fees were raging in the background but I didn't particularly care – I was having a lovely time partying in east London instead.

Still, the man I was seeing had been going to the protests and was incredibly enthusiastic about them. One day, he texted me to say that he had somehow ended up on the UCL campus, where students had started an occupation. It was, he explained, unbelievably fun and I needed to come down and join him.

My plan for that evening had been to go to the opening of a new stall in Selfridges, where a friend was DJing and, more importantly, where the champagne would be free. The weather was mild that day and I had been considering walking to Oxford Street; since UCL was in Euston and thus on the way, I agreed to drop by.

I stuffed a floor-length dress and some heels in my handbag and started walking. I do not remember much about what happened after that. All I know is that I never made it to Selfridges; that I shared an inflatable mattress that night with Ash Sarkar, who would then become a friend and a famous media commentator, and that I texted my housemates the next day to tell them that they should come join me.

A day later, my two French housemates, the man I was seeing and I, none of whom studied at UCL, formally moved into the UCL occupation. It is unclear how much any of us cared about the trebling of tuition fees at the start. The man I was seeing enjoyed having an audience at all times; I had been getting tired of hipsters and longed for a change of scenery; my housemates usually followed me wherever I went. Still, we took part in meetings, protests and direct action, and to this day, it is still possible to find news pieces calling me 'UCL student and activist Marie Le

Conte'. Looking more broadly, what was interesting about these protests was that we were all from the first generation to get online and, as a result, organically took our activism to social media.

'The protests that took place last week weren't organised by any conventional political organisation, but they managed to mobilise youngsters in towns and cities from Bournemouth to Edinburgh,' a BBC reporter wrote that month. 'It was run through social networking websites, with little centralised control.

'This DIY radicalism has its own news channels, on Facebook pages and Twitter accounts and blogs, leaving the traditional news organisations and political commentators looking in from the outside.'

Though occupations happened in dozens of camp- uses across Britain, UCL's was the one that made the most noise in the mainstream press. This was largely thanks to the expertise of one Jessica (Jess) Riches, who also joined the movement fairly randomly. Though she did study at the university, she'd never been especially political; like many of us, she fell into the occupation quite randomly, then it changed her life.

'It was incredibly organic at the time,' she told me in an email. 'We were all there with something to be angry about, a few of us joined the "media working group" and as someone who had done a lot of tweeting and Facebooking and blogging as part of my many unpaid internships, it made sense for me to do that. I'm quite an obsessive person so I took this role to heart, and because we were in London, we got quite a lot of media attention at this being some "new form of protest".

'I think our social accounts were definitely a part of showing that this was a coherent, coordinated movement and forcing a narrative and helping us tell our side of the story. Somewhat ironically, its real value was the mainstream media coverage it helped us to get, even if they were covering our "tools" before our cause. It was weird because none of us were conscious that we were doing something particularly innovative at first, this was just us communicating in the way we were used to with a more direct focus.'

Since most of us were already using social media anyway, it made sense to use it to talk about the protests we were organising and what ended up happening on those protests. Because technology wasn't quite what it is today, a lot of it involved some creative thinking, including texting people from marches so they could use their computer at UCL to post about what we were doing. I also remember having to text a special number that would automatically post tweets to your timeline, then having to wait until getting home to find out if you had gone viral.

One of my favourite bits of online mischief was *Sukey*, a website created by a handful of the most tech-minded people at the occupation. The police had decided early on in 2010 that the best way to deal with us was to 'kettle' us, which meant encircling us in the street and forbidding us from leaving. Protestors were frequently left in the cold and rain for hours on end, with no bathroom, food or drinks. *Sukey* was launched to prevent this from happening.

Inspired by the nursery rhyme – 'Polly put the kettle on [...] Sukey take it off again' – the website's aim was straightforward: it told protesters on the streets where police officers were so they could not be taken by surprise in small side streets, bridges or cul-de-sacs. People would walk around central London and text the *Sukey* team with their updates. Then, the activists at *Sukey* HQ would update their real-time map of where police were, or send automated text updates to those with older phones. It was a game of cat and mouse, and the mice started winning.

✳ ✳ ✳

I had to take a break from writing this because it made me unbearably sad. The memories I was sharing were happy ones but, knowing what would come next, it felt hard to remain chipper. I wanted to talk about the student occupation because it was emblematic of a generation that had grown up online, but also because

I see it as the embodiment of the flatness of the internet we now live in. It isn't just that we are all together, all the time; having grown up online means that every single version of us exists simultaneously, preserved in amber and exhibited for all to see.

It is suffocating.

After the UCL occupation, most students went back to their university life; about two or three dozen of us remained involved in activism. There were more marches and direct action; rooms on campus were occupied and buildings were squatted. By the autumn of 2012, two years after the British government had set out to treble tuition fees, the movement was largely dead.

People like Aaron Bastani and Ash Sarkar went on to found Novara Media and remained committed radicals. Others disappeared into their PhDs and academic jobs and were never to be seen again. Some ended up selling out and getting careers in more mainstream media and politics. Well, I personally wouldn't call it selling out, but few sell-outs would. I had simply been a student journalist who'd temporarily fallen into activism then gone back to the trade I'd been studying for.

In a pre-internet world, I suspect that no one would have cared about what I'd been up to between the ages of 18 and 20; I was not famous then and I am not famous now. Young person does something then something else is hardly fascinating. The problem is that I nailed my colours to the mast when I joined Twitter as a student activist; that was the version of me that British online circles were introduced to.

Because, as we discussed earlier, a lot of your online presence is dictated by your beliefs and special interests, I was not seen as a young French woman who, among other things, happened to be stridently left-wing. Instead, I was a strident left-winger who happened to be a young French woman.

I tweeted about left-wing politics and so did the people who followed me; I followed them back and we talked and joked and argued about left-wing politics together. Our community had been formed because we'd all occupied our universities in 2010, but that was always going to be transient. When we collectively graduated and took different paths, these online spaces began to crumble.

Some, like Jess, decided to leave altogether: 'I was always aware that I had established my very limited social media platform by being politically active and protesting a lot,' she told me. 'When I stopped being as active in that world (not because I cared any less, but because of personal circumstances and mental health issues, as well as not being a student with endless hours for it anymore), I felt like no one would really care about what I had to say outside of that. And in a way I felt ashamed and guilty for becoming less active in that world and didn't want to draw attention to my absence.'

I stayed on Twitter and did not give it much thought. I turned 21, 22, 23 and my career went from odd shifts at various newspapers to increasingly steady roles. I evolved and changed because it is what you do when you are that age. I got a full-time job as a political journalist when I was 23 and suddenly my tweeting could no longer be as self-indulgent as it once had been. I could still be silly, of course, but I took my job seriously.

When Jeremy Corbyn was elected Labour leader in 2016, I did not welcome him with open arms. I did not think he would be sharp enough to get the party into government and some of his policy stances, on foreign affairs and at home, struck me as desperately unpopular. It shouldn't have mattered; I was a reasonably junior journalist and no one had to care about my views. Instead, all hell broke loose. I received abuse online every day; people tweeted mean things at me and about me, about me being a repulsive sell-out and careerist scum. People who were still friends with me on Facebook would take to Twitter to discuss how much they hated me, day after day after day after day. People I had cooked for and received in my home blocked me so they could talk about me without giving me a chance to respond.

In hindsight, I am not sure what hurt more. The real-life friends who denounced me to keep their social standing in left-wing circles pierced my heart, but the strangers who felt betrayed by the fact I had changed baffled me even more. They did not know me and I did not know them; why would they care? Was I, a person among so many others, not allowed to change? Was I really accountable to *them*?

Much as it was painful at the time, my bruised feelings aren't the reason I am bringing this up. Instead, I find the reasoning of the people who loathed me worth exploring. The extent to which they could not stand me makes me think that their sense of betrayal was entirely sincere. They thought me one of them even if they did not know me, and me getting a career in political journalism felt personal.

On the internet, people are not allowed to change and time is not allowed to pass. I wonder if it is because everything we have ever posted on, say, Twitter or Facebook will still be there by default, unless we made the active decision to delete our archives. People confronted me by pulling up posts from 2011 and comparing them to things I had posted in 2017.

The change in tone and opinion looked jarring because the old posts and the new tweets looked exactly the same, and the old posts were so easy to find that they still felt fresh. They made me look hypocritical and inconsistent, when it is entirely normal to have changed quite a lot between the ages of 19 and 25. That did not stop me from falling into a bit of an identity crisis at the time: was I really a terrible person? Did I really have no moral compass? The only thing that brought me solace was to eventually be able to look back at my tweets from 2017 and realise that I have changed a lot since then, again. The internet is flat and time is not allowed to pass, and the problem is not me. In fact, it is an issue that keeps cropping up in public discourse, because we have no idea what to do with the things people posted online when they were younger. At time of writing, the most recent example is Ollie Robinson, a bowler for England's cricket team. Currently 27, Robinson was found to have posted racist and sexist tweets in 2012 and 2013, and was suspended from the team by the English Cricket Board. This was his statement: 'On the biggest day of my career so far, I am embarrassed by the racist and sexist tweets that I posted over eight years ago, which have today become public. I want to make it clear that I'm not racist and I'm not sexist.

'I deeply regret my actions, and I am ashamed of making such remarks. I was thoughtless and irresponsible, and regardless of my state of mind at the time, my actions were inexcusable. Since that period, I have matured as a person and fully regret the tweets.'

In the days following the original revelations,

Culture Secretary Oliver Dowden intervened to defend Robinson, others backed the ECB's decision and we got no closer to deciding how we, as a society, want to deal with stories like these. There is little point in spending time discussing what Robinson did or did not post and how much he did or did not change after he made those posts, because it is not very relevant. After all, I used Ollie Robinson's example but I could have used a million others – it is a genre of stories that now crops up every other month, week or even day. Person is in the public eye; person turns out to have said offensive things online in the past; current beliefs and character of person are debated; the world moves on.

In a way, it is easier when the person turns out not to have changed at all and to still hold objectionable views. It is what happened to Jared O'Mara, the former Labour MP for Sheffield Hallam. In 2017, a few months after he was elected, a website published a number of comments he had made on forums between 2002 and 2004, when he was in his early twenties. The jokes were sexist and homophobic but they were old – was he still the same person now? As it turned out, he was; a few days later, offensive comments he had made in 2016 were revealed. The case had barely been opened and now it was closed. Though O'Mara was never quite popular enough to fit the meme, he was what we could call Milkshake Duck-adjacent.

If you've not come across it before, the 'Milkshake Duck' started with this tweet, posted by @pixelatedboat in 2016: 'The whole internet loves Milkshake Duck, a lovely duck that drinks milkshakes! *5 seconds later* We regret to inform you the duck is racist'. It deftly poked fun at a dynamic that had already become ubiquitous online by the mid-2010s. Someone would gain instant popularity by going viral for some reason; people would dig into their social media profiles and find offensive things; the person would be denounced then returned to obscurity. Rinse, repeat.

By about 2017, that cycle had become so well-known that 'Milkshake Duck' was widely adopted as a phrase and even got turned into a verb. If someone 'milkshake ducked', it meant that they'd had their 15 seconds of fame and it had ended poorly. It's a catchy way to talk about a straightforward phenomenon. The problem, however, is that unearthing old offensive posts often turns into a more complex quandary, as evidenced by Ollie Robinson's case. Off the top of my head, these are the questions that hide behind most of these cases:

How young was the person when they made the offensive remarks? Is it old enough to know better? Should you definitely excuse what someone said before they were 18? If not, which things are so offensive that saying them while underage remains a red flag? If they said the offensive things at 20, do we decide they were old enough to know better or still young enough to deserve a pass? How about 21? 23? 25? Is there an age at which the person just becomes fully responsible for what they said?

What if they said offensive things at 26 but they are now 12 years older? Has enough time passed? If they said offensive things at 19 but they are now only 23, can we be sure they have changed since then? Humour used to be a lot coarser ten years ago, especially online – where is the line between jokes that have aged poorly and remarks that are simply awful? Does it matter where the line is? Should it?

How can someone show that they have changed since they posted these offensive things? Who gets to decide that they have changed enough? Are there things so offensive that the person who posted them cannot ever come back from them? If so, who gets to decide what these things are? In any case, how should someone atone for what they said? Is an apology enough? If not, what else should they do?

There are no set answers to any of these questions, which means that we are yet to agree on a set way to deal with people who posted offensive things online when they were younger. It is, after all, a new phenomenon; if you were born before 1985 – 1980 at a stretch – it would not have been possible for you to misspend your youth on the internet. It's a new problem and there is no way for us all to agree on how to deal with it, because every case is a little bit different, but the vast majority of them live in a bit of a grey area.

An adjacent issue is that of people being famous for one thing but having controversial beliefs in another area of life. If you are left-wing, should you buy the books of an author who has donated money to the Conservative party? If you are passionate about trans rights, should you pay to go to the gigs of a gender critical singer? Should you support an actor by watching his movies if he is an anti-vaxxer? These are not entirely new quandaries, as famous people have always found a way to make their most strongly-held views public, but the internet has pushed these questions a step further. It isn't about what is said anymore, what doesn't get mentioned can be just as important.

If you are a woman and a feminist, would you buy the books of a male author who remained conspic-uously silent when #MeToo exploded? If you care about American politics and the lives of people who live in the US, would you pay to go to the gigs of a singer who refused to comment on Donald Trump's most callous policies? Should you support an actor by watching his movies if he did not post about Black Lives Matter even once? These are all hypothetical, though one real-life example can be singer-songwriter Taylor

Swift, whose refusal to talk about politics up until 2018 became increasingly untenable. She eventually broke her silence before the midterms, releasing a statement: 'In the past I've been reluctant to publicly voice my political opinions, but due to several events in my life and in the world in the past two years, I feel very differently about that now. I believe in the fight for LGBTQ rights, and that any form of discrimination based on sexual orientation or gender is WRONG. I believe that the systemic racism we still see in this country towards people of color is terrifying, sickening and prevalent.'

It was interesting because this expectation for entertainers to speak up was not always there. Political and apolitical celebrities could co-exist in peace and, perhaps more importantly, get to decide which one they wanted to be. That is no longer the case, especially for famous people wishing to appeal to a younger audience. If you ask certain middle-aged commentators why this change took place, they will probably tell you that snowflake, socialist millennials refuse to get triggered by views they disagree with, or something along those lines.

Though I do believe it is a generational cleavage, I think – try to contain your shock – that the internet we grew up with is to blame. If you grew up online at a certain time, most of who you are will be out there in the open. Your identity, your passions and opinions will be publicly available, or at least somewhere out there if people know where to look. It seems logical, then, that we would expect a similar level of openness from those we want to idolise and support financially. The argument that it doesn't matter what someone thinks of trans people if their day job is to write children's books doesn't hold water. Our entire selves are out there and theirs must be too, and if they are, they can and will be judged in consequence.

It's not really a political statement, or at least it doesn't feel like one; if I'm being honest, writing this chapter is what forced me to think about where this difference in expectations came from. Until then, I'd simply taken it as a part of life. Still – established, real-life celebrities are only the tip of the iceberg. As Milkshake Duck shows, we expect this level of openness from just about everyone. It can be exhausting; I remember once retweeting something from a pro-immigration advocate and being told that I should undo my retweet as that person was a transphobe. Did it really matter if our beliefs aligned on immigration, the topic the original tweet was about? I ask not as a rhetorical question, but because I sincerely do not know. Does it?

This goes back to the many unanswered – and often unanswerable – questions about offensive posts from the past. We were never meant to have our entire selves, past and present, strewn across the internet. People are not only different depending on who they are talking to; they also evolve and change with time and must be allowed to quietly leave their old selves behind. This is especially true in their formative years: who doesn't change radically between their teenage years and adulthood?

It is a tension that feels especially acute for those of us who were born between the mid-1980s and mid-1990s. If you were born before that decade, you were already at least a young adult by the time the internet really started to take shape. You also remembered a time before it existed, which presumably shaped your relationship with it. If you were born afterwards, you never experienced life offline.

By the time you began your teenage years, the internet had already become a close enough version of what it is today. Crucially, more or less everyone was on there already by the time you joined, which made it an entirely different space altogether. Of course, this doesn't mean that the people born around those ten years are the only ones to ever get caught out by stupid or mindless things they posted online. Mistakes are what makes us human; some people will always be especially unlucky, others certainly had it coming, and so on. Still, our fate felt especially cruel, particularly in regards to work and the barriers between our personal and professional selves being removed without our consent. An example that comes to mind is the internship I did at a publication in 2013. On my first day I turned up still so drunk from the night before that I could barely walk straight. By the end of the second day I had developed an all-encompassing crush on one of the editors, as is customary. Another editor always took what felt like days to reply to my emails – presumably because he had a real job to do – and by the end of the first week he had become my nemesis.

All of this was, of course, documented on my Twitter account. The highs and lows of my fortnight working as an intern were shared with an audience of a few hundred people. Because my account was still anonymous and I'd never named the media organisation, I didn't stop to think about whether this live tweeting was in any way a good idea. The suckerpunch came on my last day, when a senior editor kindly agreed to talk to me about the work I had done in those few weeks.

She had overall been happy with me and thought I had done my job well. The only thing, she told me as we both left the meeting room, was that I should be more careful about what I posted on Twitter. I smiled meekly because I didn't know what else to do; my heart stopped for what felt like hours. Somehow, I didn't radically alter the output of my account after that, maybe because I was young, or maybe because I wanted to remain in denial. Around four years later, I woke up hungover one morning and was gripped by paranoia, as sometimes happens when you have drunk too much the night before. I logged into Facebook and looked through the entire history of my wall, all eight or nine years of it, and deleted everything I thought could be controversial.

I then did the same to my Instagram feed and paid a few dollars for a company to delete most of my old tweets. It took about five hours in total; by the end, I felt like a weight had been lifted from my shoulders. My career had started in earnest by that point and as of that day, I no longer had to worry about it getting sidetracked by old posts. Thinking about it now mostly makes me sad. I had managed to build a sprawling archive of words, messages and pictures spanning about a decade of my life and I destroyed it all in one afternoon.

It almost feels like the worst of both worlds, as my past has been present enough online to still torment me in the present. Everything I like is gone, and everything I hated will, through the memories of people who hate me, live on forever. It is something Jess brought up as well, without me even asking her about it.

'I am painfully aware that most of the correspondence from my relationships in my most formative years is gone, and the photos too. I know it was only ever supposed to be ephemeral, no one promised me otherwise, but the point is that when you're a teenager you think that nothing matters but also that it will last forever,' she wrote to me.

'I never put all of that into MySpace or MSN or Hotmail or Facebook thinking, "this is for safe keeping", but I made hugely significant memories on those platforms, memories I will never be able to access.

'I'm really bitter about this and exhausted just thinking about all of the steps I'll have to take if I do want to maintain or archive anything I've housed online. And I know I don't have to, it really is just digital debris, but it's who I am. I lose sleep thinking about how I'll never be able to find anything again, and then eventually when I'm dead my potential future kids will have to wade through administrative screengrabs and landscape photos and so many nudes just to find a picture of their mum having fun in her twenties. I think about my future kids every time I take a nude. It really kills the vibe.'

Again, the worst of both worlds. Though all the texts, MSN messages and various DMs we have sent over the years have long disappeared, any stray tasteless joke left somewhere googleable can ruin our lives. Across countless white-collar industries, all our current and potential future bosses share the same spaces as us; they may not always make themselves known, but we cannot forget that they are there.

Our colleagues are online and if we become even somewhat friendly with them we will end up following each other on social media. Every time I post a nice and tipsy picture of myself in a short party dress on Instagram, there is a chance it will be liked by the newseditor of a newspaper. Every time I post a tweet analysing an event in British politics, my high school friends will see it. The internet is flat and all the barriers have fallen.

It's not only about the past or the present; because our past posts hang over us like a sword, we must always remember that what we post today may bring us embarrassment tomorrow. I take pole dancing classes and I love them but I hesitate to get involved in the pole dancing community, not because I fear that it would hurt my career now, but because I have no idea what my career will be like in a decade.

Will I be in a job where it is frowned upon to do acrobatics in your underwear on and around a 50mm stainless steel pole? I have no idea, but it seems safer not to risk it, even if I want to. I owe it to my future self, whoever she may be. Well, I don't know who she is but I do spend a lot of time thinking about her; if I'm embarrassed by my past self today, what am I doing today that will embarrass me in a year, five years, twenty years?

The internet is flat because there is no longer space

between all the different versions of ourselves. I exist online as a 29-year-old but I am also on there as a 17-year-old music fan and a 20-year-old activist. Like millions of Ebenezer Scrooges, we are visited by ghosts of the past, present and future, and we must calibrate our lives as a result.

The internet is flat and I worry that it is making us flatter. If we must be everything to everyone all the time and every iteration of ourselves can come back to haunt us, can we really be our full selves? It feels especially perverse because the early internet allowed us to experiment and mess up and change and disappear. That was the entire point. Instead, an air of paranoia now pervades our online experiences and there is no real line between our online selves and our real-life selves anymore. If you go out dancing and get very drunk and the club uploads a picture of you being very drunk and for some reason it goes viral, what do you do? If you went to protests some years ago and carried banners with inflammatory slogans and the pictures remain online, what can you do?

It's not just that the internet has made us worry about what we do online and how it comes across; thanks to the advance of technology, whatever happens offline can also be plastered across the internet, with very real consequences. There is nowhere to hide.

An example that comes to mind is both mundane

and maddening. A man named Emmanuel Cafferty was driving his company truck in California; it was a warm day and his arm was hanging out the window. A Black Lives Matter protest had happened nearby and some people were walking back, still holding placards. Someone took a picture of Cafferty and posted it on Twitter; according to them, the driver had been making an 'OK' gesture with his fingers, a symbol used by white supremacists.

The tweet went viral and Cafferty lost his job. It didn't matter that he was a Mexican American man himself and was just cracking his knuckles, or that he didn't know the 'OK' sign had become code for a racist slogan: 'I don't know how long it's going to take me to get over this, but to lose your dream job for playing with your fingers, that's a hard pill to swallow,' he told NBC 7 some days later.

There are many things to be said about this incident, but the one I always come back to is the most straightforward one. Emmanuel Cafferty was a spectacularly unlucky man and the internet ruined his life for no reason. It was him yesterday, it could be any of us tomorrow. Were this a different book, this would be the time for me to talk about surveillance, big data and the large companies ensuring that we have no privacy left. It's not something I really want to get into, because if you haven't read about these topics again and again over the past few years, where have you been? Instead, I would like to talk about something more uncomfortable. There is too much information about too many of us currently floating online and it isn't just terrible, it is also unbelievably fun.

I love googling people more than I love most other things in life and I'm sure that I'm not the only one. I love googling people I meet through work and I love googling people I see on television; I love googling people I go on dates with and I love googling people who went to the same school as me.

There is no such thing as a true stranger anymore; in especially obsessive moments, I have tracked down the family members of people with little internet presence in the hope that they shared pictures and facts about their relative. I was banned from the fan forum of the Horrors because I managed to find the Gumtree ad two of the members had posted because they were looking for a third housemate.

I wonder if this is one of the most tangible cleavages between our generation and the ones who came before us. We are, I suppose, very entitled; not because we feel we deserve jobs or houses or pats on the head when we achieve something, but because we have had access to an intoxicating amount of information about others for most of our lives. If someone exists and I am aware of them, I do feel I deserve the right to find out everything

I want about them. What was that stranger like when they were at university? What does their partner look like? What music do they listen to? Why shouldn't I get to know these things if they are all there, especially if you know where to look?

I wish I could say the thrill came from knowing it was an intrusive thing to do but in truth, I am so used to it that it just feels normal. Instead, I feel bereft and robbed when I google someone and they turn out not to be very online at all. We are all in this together, or at least we should be. Maybe it is hypocritical, given how wounding it feels when people drag up parts of your past without your consent. Maybe we are all crabs in a bucket; if I'm not allowed privacy and relative anonymity, then no one else should have it.

We are watching each other and being watched constantly, and when we are not, we must still act like we are in case someone does end up watching us at some point in the future. We were very free and then we were not. We could be a dozen different people at the same time and now we must remain one and the same for all eternity, or face having to answer for our changes to people we know and people we do not; people who mean well and people who do not. We are trapped and there is no way out, because at heart, we know that we are also the ones doing the watching.

It is a cruel bargain, because free and unlimited

information about everyone around you is too appealing an offer to turn down, no matter the price. In our defence, we weren't even given a choice, not really; we plastered ourselves across the internet then the internet was turned against us. We simply grabbed what we could in return.

Never Stopped Me Dreaming

It can be hard to write about the internet because the internet tricks us into thinking that all our experiences are both unique and universal. I am writing this for and on behalf of people whose lives were quite similar to mine, but how many people is that? They are people born, roughly, between the mid-1980s and mid-1990s, but not all the people born between those dates will identify with it.

Someone like my old school friend Morgane, for example, would fit the age criteria but would probably not relate to most of these essays, because she never was that online when we were teenagers. How many people will see themselves in what I'm writing? I'm asking because there is something I would like to discuss but I'm not sure how relatable it is. It is nestled here, between longer chapters, for the very simple reason that it is not something I was aware of when I pitched this book and all the themes in it.

Around six months after I wrote the proposal for *Escape*, I was diagnosed with ADHD (attention deficit hyperactivity disorder). It wasn't a huge surprise; my appointment with the psychiatrist was cut short because my symptoms were, if anything, too obvious. I started writing this book three months later, at a point when I was still mulling over my diagnosis and what it meant in the context of my relationship with the internet.

ADHD manifests differently in different people; in my case, the one symptom that sets me apart from those with neurotypical brains is my tendency to hyperfocus. This is how *Additude*, a website for people with ADHD, describes it: 'Hyperfocus refers to an intense fixation on an interest or activity for an extended period of time. People who experience hyperfocus often become so engrossed they block out the world around them.'

It can be hard to accurately convey just how engrossed I can become in something. Once, when I was 16, I decided to teach myself HTML and rebuild my music website from scratch. I started at around 11am and finished after midnight; in that time, I did not eat, drink or go to the bathroom.

At 23, I was teaching myself about British politics

and I became obsessed with Peter Mandelson; I watched every documentary on the New Labour years I could find in the space of about two weeks. I downloaded the audiobook of his memoirs, read out by him, and listened to it from the moment I woke up until the moment I got to my desk at work. I listened to it during lunch breaks, which I chose to spend alone, and I listened to it again the moment I left my work at the end of the day.

I realise that people who do not have ADHD can also be very passionate about things or topics or people, but the difference is that I do not get to pick what I hyperfocus on. My brain sometimes feels like a Venus fly trap; an insect or a bit of pollen will land on me and get glued in and I will have no choice but to absorb it. It can be maddening; there are things I do not want to obsess over, either because I do not have the time or cannot be bothered, but my brain does not give me a choice.

Once I have fallen for something, I will not be able to think about anything else. It is a very physical feeling; if I try to do something else or even let my mind stray for a bit, my body will feel tense and uncomfortable. At risk of overdosing on metaphors, it is like being a magnet living in a world of magnets. If I get too close to one, I can try very hard not to stick to it, but the effort will always be obvious to me because the attraction does not go away.

ESCAPE

When I fall into one of these spirals, my brain becomes a deep black void, desperate to hoover up every single piece of information it can find on that one thing, topic or person. It can be exhilarating or exhausting; often it is both. It should go without saying that, when this happens the internet becomes my best friend and worst enabler when this happens.

Unstoppable force, meet endless depths.

Over the years I have absorbed so many facts that even thinking about it makes my head spin. I have read millions and millions of words, hunched over my laptop, lying in bed, sitting on the bus, unable to sleep, unwilling to stand up and go for lunch, unbothered by my full bladder. I have spent days and weeks stuck to my screen, googling page after page and clicking from one website to another then another, incapable of stopping.

I am mentioning this now because I had no other choice; once again, I have been engulfed by an obsession and I cannot think or write about anything else. I may as well tell you about it now because there is nothing else happening in my brain at the moment. It will temporarily anchor this book at a specific point in time but, well, it's that or nothing.

Three weeks ago, in the middle of June 2021, England played against Croatia in the Euros. I didn't watch the game – I had a pole dancing lesson that clashed with it and I didn't want to cancel it. Also, I had never cared about the Euros before, but was vaguely considering keeping an eye on them as a way to distract myself from the ongoing pandemic. I had, after all, had a wonderful time watching the World Cup in 2018 despite knowing nothing about football and wasn't against the idea of repeating the experiment.

I watched England's next game then the game after that; I watched all of France's games until we lost to Switzerland in the round of 16. When that happened, I jokingly tweeted that I would have to wholeheartedly support England instead as I had no other choice. "Jokingly".

England played against Denmark last night and I could not focus on anything else for the entire day. My blood was pumping from the moment I woke up until the game ended. I woke up this morning and as I walked to work, I listened to 'Three Lions' and silently mouthed along to the lyrics, getting teary at the mention of Gareth Southgate. I had never knowingly heard 'Three Lions' until five days earlier. I didn't watch the first England game because I couldn't be bothered to move my pole dancing lesson. It was three weeks ago.

Today, I sat at my desk for three hours and I couldn't write because all I could think about was the England squad. I googled them all again, one by one, despite having already googled them all at least three or four times each. I scrolled through dozens of posts on the team's Twitter and the team's Instagram; I went on all the players' individual profiles and I looked at every picture and read every caption.

Every time I tried to do something else, my heart rate got faster and a knot started to grow in my throat. Every time I took 30 seconds out to reply to an email, I rewarded myself by looking at pictures of the players hugging on the pitch. It was a problem until it wasn't; I was driving myself to insanity by not being able to write about the internet until I realised that football fitted perfectly into my writing about the internet.

I'm an obsessive person and at a young age was handed a portal into a world where all the information I could ever want was immediately available to me. What could possibly be more relevant? What gets trickier, however, is attempting to separate the chicken from the egg. Did I grow up online because my ADHD means I am a naturally obsessive person? Were my more obsessive traits worsened by my access to the internet from a tender age? It also seems worth looking at the bigger picture: many people I spoke to for this book have ADHD, autism or both. Is that a coincidence?

A lot of the early internet was based on common interests and a lot of the people who built that early internet were spectacularly nerdy. Diagnosing them with autism or ADHD from afar would be a step too far, but it is surely uncontroversial to state what they built was a haven for neurodivergent people.

Suddenly you could meet people like you in the safety of your own home and throw yourself two-footed into whatever passion you had. Popular kids were not there to torment you and there was no imperative for you to fit in; instead, you could build communities around the quirks that made you unpopular in real life. If there was something you wanted to spend days and nights reading about then discussing with others, you could do it. If your brain woke up one day and decided you no longer cared about that topic, you could move on and never look back – it was salvation, it was heaven. It is also why I have a tendency to anthropomorphise the internet. I do not quite see 'online' as a person but I do absolutely think about online as a fixed entity. When a website I like changes, I take it as a personal slight; when something very good or very bad happens to me, I post about it online before texting my friends and family. I feel sincere nostalgia when I look at a page I hadn't looked at in years; there are corners of the internet that calm me and make me feel at home.

Perhaps anthropomorphise is the wrong word, then. I think of the internet as a place, my own personal Narnia. Because my life is ruled by these intense interests that take over my brain for days and months at a time, and because the internet is where I go to try and quench my unquenchable thirst, it has always felt like a very special place. It is intimate and personal; I come in begging for facts on football, New Labour politics, dinosaurs and the different ethnic groups in Russia and it gives them to me.

My obsessions make me who I am and the internet helps me deal with these obsessions; because of my ADHD, the internet is who I am. It is the place where I have found communities that helped me feel like I belonged but more importantly, the internet is, in itself, my community.

How many people feel the same? When I am writing this, am I putting words on the thoughts and feelings of millions of people? Thousands? Dozens? We all live here now and our experiences are both unique and universal. I'm going to google pictures of Jordan Pickford again.

We Are Your Friends

I have always enjoyed lying. I lie to make people's lives easier, as well as my own; I lie because I like a shortcut and telling the truth often complicates matters. I never lie about the big things; the best lies are, in my opinion, the ones small enough that, even if you are caught, will not matter a whole lot. Lying is fun but only when it is not very important. This is why it puzzles me that when someone asks me why and how I got to writing about British politics as a French woman, I always tell the truth. It is a question that comes up often, which I cannot even resent because it is a reasonable query. People have asked me that question on the radio and on television; in front of audiences of 20 and audiences of 200.

It would be so easy for me to lie and invent something

both wry and compelling. Instead, I have always told the truth. How did I get interested in British politics? Because I wanted to get laid.

It was May 2010 and the last day of my first year at university. There was a man I had slept with once and wanted to sleep with again because he was very beautiful; he was the guitarist of an indie rock band, as they often were, and was playing in a pub that night. I dragged some friends there and we got very drunk; to celebrate the start of the summer, I bought everyone shots and, for every shot they drank, I drank one as well.

After the gig, the beautiful man came up to me and, touching my arm, told me he was going to have an after party at his house and that I should come. My friends left because they did not know anyone going to the after party and assumed that I would be otherwise engaged from the moment we got there.

I left with his friends and realised my mistake once we reached his house. He had started talking to a woman who was not me but had clearly captured his attention, and there was little I could do about it. I looked around and it hit me – really hit me – that I was 18 years old, in a house full of people in their late twenties, none of whom I knew, and that I did not know how to get home because the Underground had stopped.

I kept on drinking.

Eventually I noticed that the television was on and, out of sheer awkwardness, went to watch it. It was around 2am and the night of the 2010 general election. I had no idea what I was looking at – I knew the party leaders' names and not much else – but it was oddly captivating. What even was a 'hung Parliament'? It took me about an hour to figure it out.

Somehow, I ended up becoming the political correspondent of the house party. I sat by the television with my bottle of wine – no glass – and whenever a seat changed hands I informed my audience. At some point the beautiful man, who was very dim, asked me what a hung Parliament was; I explained it to him and he went to repeat it, word for word, to the woman he had chosen for the night.

In the end I stayed by that screen until about 7am, by which point more or less everyone had left or gone to bed. I went to take the Tube and was oddly chipper, partly because of the two or three bottles of wine I had drunk over the space of 12 hours, but mostly because I had found a new passion.

That is the story of how I got into British politics; I have told it to anyone who has asked, from interviewers and MPs to future bosses and people I have only just met. It is quite embarrassing and deeply unprofessional, but it is the truth. I could lie, but for some reason I don't. Well, it is partly a lie because it is most of the story but not all of it. The events of 2010 marked the beginning of my interest in British politics; my obsession only really started in the summer of 2015.

I had, by that point, been floating around in journalism for two years. A dabbler by nature, I'd been working across different desks at different newspapers; none of my roles had been entirely about politics, but some had been Westminster-adjacent. I helped out with coverage of the 2015 election whenever I could but was only ever an afterthought. On the night itself, I was put in charge of making memes for a newspaper's Twitter account.

While this was happening in real life, my online life was beginning to take a turn. I had been on Tumblr for many happy years already, but had somehow ended up in the 'lolitics' corner, where young people made increasingly bizarre and niche memes about British politics. It is very hard to explain lolitics now, because so many of the posts were so deranged that talking about them would not do them justice. Instead, here is something Tumblr user Cones Hotline – yes, named after the obscure John Major-era policy – posted in 2015:

'I'm so glad that the way people get interested in historical lolitics seems to have remained constant throughout the years. it starts innocently enough.

first you become interested in modern happenings
– in ed miliband the precious cinnamon roll, in
davie cam's ham plan, in nick clegg's sad face.
you begin your journey backwards and discover
the world of new labour. the psychodrama, the
ruined friendships, the spectre of tony blair
wandering around naked everywhere. you go
further backwards, praying to the cones hotline,
discovering the thatcher years and the hot mess
that was the sdp-liberal alliance. you watch a
lot of spitting image. you talk in hushed breaths
of the 1981 labour deputy leadership conetest.
you realise nothing in this life can live up to the
owen/steel fishing trip and wonder why steely
didn't just push owen off the boatever backwards
now. the 70s, 60s – the splits! the screeching over
europe! the repressed homosexuality! you make
a shrine to rinka the dog, unfairly taken from this
world before her time, in your room. backwards.
the 50s. the 40s. the attlee government. you paper
the walls of your house with pictures of nye bevan.
you scream in terror at herbert morrison's quiff.
backwards! stanley baldwin! my goodness, you
love stanley baldwin. you could post about him
for hours. backwards. you're shipping gladsraeli.
goddamnit. you're shipping glads-fucking-raeli.
you watch documentaries about robert peel and

love it. what next? where else is there to go? surely there must be depths you have not plunged yet but the best part is – all these interests stack. you don't replace one with another. oh no. you're left with intimate knowledge of hundreds of political figures and events. you could shitpost about them for years. i should know - *i already have'*

This is, to a frightening extent, what happened to me. At first, I enjoyed the memes about the Labour leadership contest; though I was following more serious news about the party's woes, weird and oddly astute online posts were always going to appeal to me more. As someone who was still a relative newcomer at the time, they also helped me get to grips with the more obscure political figures.

I could have read lengthy magazine profiles and interviews in Sunday papers but they weren't quite the same; instead, shitposters taught me about British politics. I cannot thank them enough; had it not been for Tumblr, my interest in Westminster probably would not have turned into a career.

It is not something I talk about often because it is a little bit shameful; I am both an adult and a journalist, did I really have to get into politics in this way? Could I not have read the *New Statesman* and listened to the *Today* programme like everyone else? But then I go back and look at those Tumblrs again and realise that there is nothing to be ashamed of. This, for example, was posted by Cones in June 2015:

'would the labour leadership candidates hold your hair while you vomited outside a club: the real question that needs to be answered

andy burnham: as a sturdy liverpudlian, andy would definitely hold your hair while you vomited outside a club. he would also call you a cab afterwards and/or offer to take you to a&e where he can tut about the queues that are still present thanks to that mean old jeremy hunt

chuka umunna: would not hold your hair while you vomited outside a club. he would get his immaculate designer suit dirty. probably would get one of his ~people~ to assist you though, then give you his card

yvette cooper: would probably hold your hair while you vomited outside a club, but in a kind of stiff way, so you know she's honestly trying but bits of loose hair keep getting drenched with vom chunks

dan jarvis: dan jarvis would not only hold your hair while you vomited outside a club, he would then pick you up and carry you, bridal style, all the way home and tuck you into bed. unfortunately this would only happen in your dreams as he has declined to go to the club with you and the other candidates in the first place. rip in peace my son

liz kendall: would be long gone before you even began to vomit outside the club, ditching you and your mates to hook up with that smiley dude named tony you never liked. you are stuck with your true gal pals stella creasy and gloria de piero who would never betray in this manner

tristram hunt: would respond to you vomiting outside a club by going off on a spiel about the victorian architecture of the club itself and how it was once a scene of chartist protest. then he'd walk away humming to himself about appealing to voters who shop at john lewis. this isn't what you wanted. this isn't what you wanted at all'

If you remember these candidates, do you not agree that these descriptions are spot on? If you don't, do you not feel that reading this gave you a decent idea of who these people are? Their politics are not mentioned once but that doesn't really matter, because politics is, at heart, about people, their personalities and how they are perceived by the world at large. I should know; I wrote a whole book about that once. You can read it after this one if you like, it's pretty good. Anyway, this was not my point; my point is that, like Cones predicted, I started reading Tumblr posts about contemporary politics and slowly found myself wanting more. I decided I had to learn about the New Labour years and so I read Alastair Campbell and Peter Mandelson's memoirs; I fell further down into the rabbit hole and I watched documentaries about Labour under Michael Foot.

My thirst for political knowledge still wasn't quenched so I started learning about the Conservatives; I read about the reign of the Cameroons and I watched *Tory! Tory! Tory!*, about the rise of Thatcherism. In under six months, I went from someone with an interest in politics to someone who knew considerably more about politics than your average person. All of it started because Cones and her friends posted memes about Willie Whitelaw and I didn't understand them and it made me feel left out. It is, objectively, embarrassing. Still, I felt the need to bring it up because the internet has changed the way we engage with politics; my own story may be extreme but it is not unique. Politics is now a community like any other; though party members and assorted nerds have always existed, it used to be much harder to have such a sustained interest in current affairs.

You could go to meetings and deliver leaflets and attend party conferences but that required time and dedication. Thanks to social media in general and Twitter more specifically, anyone who wants to can now spend their waking hours opining on the ebbs and flows of Westminster. Picking a party to support or getting a job in SW1 are no longer requirements either; on political Twitter, anyone and everyone can become a wag if they so wish.

I talked about this with Josh Lowe, who is 30 and works in policy and, like me, tweets like his life depends on it. I wanted to know how he had found his way into politics and was surprised when he emailed back; as it happens, his experience very much mirrors my own, albeit without the Tumblr memes.

'My significant teenage online communities were the most basic ones for my generation: MSN messenger in the early teens, MySpace later. The former was basically a place to show off whatever very cool lyrics I had discovered that week in my display name. The latter was a place to thrust my extremely poor "solo music" on helpless friends who visited the page (think that Brighteyes synth album but terrible). All now lost in the great MySpace data wipe, like tears in rain.

'It wasn't until young adulthood, post-uni really, that the internet became a bigger part of my life than the average person. I threw myself into political Twitter, Reddit and the blogosphere (mostly as a reader, in the latter case) and in the space of maybe a year or two went from not being able to name any of the Cabinet to being conversant in a bunch of niche policy topics (education and housing originally). It was a confrontation with reality, opening up my careful, fussy little cultural world to a dizzying array of others' experiences and hard facts, from debates over trans rights to crash courses in 20th-century political history.'

(I should point out that between putting this quote in the text and returning to my Google Doc, I clicked on the mentions tab of my Twitter app and Josh was there, having just liked a tweet of mine. When I said that he tweets like his life depends on it, I meant it.)

(And since we're doing asides; I do find it amusing that the indie music-to-British-politics pipeline is so active. Who knew that so many people could be interested in both young posh white men with overinflated egos *and* slightly older posh white men with overinflated egos?)

I liked his reply because it shows that my own online obsession with politics is entirely unremarkable. Anecdotally, I know of many other people who did not have an interest in politics as teenagers and did not study it at university but, instead, somehow fell into it because of the internet.

For good or ill, politics has become a hobby like any other; it is something you can have opinions about day after day and something you can base friendships and feuds on. It can even shape your entire online personality, even if your job in real life has nothing to do with it. Cones, for example, has no interest in ever working in Westminster.

I asked her about it, because we did eventually become online friends, and this is what she told me: 'Despite the fame and fortune (someone donated £3 to me once), I eventually realised that posting pictures of David Owen's straining bosom is no way to live one's life if they don't want to end up dead in a ditch. Therefore, I decided to become an educator teaching YOUR kids! Thankfully, I am a normalish person irl so don't worry about it, folks. Anyway, like many hapless teens, I first thought how cool it would be to be an MP before swiftly deciding that no, actually, it would be awful.'

Because the bar for involvement in political discourse has been lowered dramatically, anyone can now join in; because the internet makes it easy for people to become utterly obsessed with something, many people have. In some ways it has been a very good thing; as Josh pointed out, it is now possible to learn about any topic you can possibly be interested in, no matter how niche or technical. There are experts everywhere and many of them are open about their work and happy to interact with enthusiastic amateurs.

The horizontal nature of the internet in general and Twitter specifically also means that we can now hear from more people than ever. From race and gender to class and feminism, people with relevant life experiences and incisive opinions can now make themselves heard, even if they do not have a platform in the media or elsewhere.

The #MeToo movement of 2017 was a good example of this; suddenly, women of all shapes, ages, races, backgrounds and sexualities were able to share what had happened to them with the world. There was no gatekeeping and no people in positions of power choosing what and who to highlight; anyone with a Facebook, Instagram or Twitter account could share their story. More broadly, traditionally marginalised communities are now able to talk back when attacked or misrepresented. They may not always win the debate in the end, as voices featured in the mainstream media still carry more weight, but they cannot be ignored.

We are, both as a bubble of nerds who like talking about politics and as a society at large, richer for it. I have read about the lives and experiences of thousands of people thanks to Twitter and know that countless others have as well. It has been eye-opening, perhaps even life-changing. Sadly, this does not mean that the internet's effect on the global political discourse has been wholly positive. Events like #MeToo and Black Lives Matter probably would not have happened without places like Twitter, Facebook and Instagram, but the same could be said of the election of Donald Trump and the global rise of the far right.

Politics was divisive, toxic and disingenuine long before the internet was invented, but throwing the worst aspects of online culture into the mix only made it worse. Because most of the people who write about politics are too old to have really grown up online, coverage of those issues has also often been lacking.

One example I come back to often is fandom, and the idea that most baffling political fights on the internet can be best understood by comparing activists, trolls and politicians to, say, One Direction groupies. An English academic has been studying the phenomenon of fandoms for several years and, conveniently, happens to be a friend of mine. Though Phoenix Andrews is, at time of writing, working on his own book on the topic, I asked him to explain what he means when he says that all politics online is fandom.

'lol Marie I can't write my book for your book,' was his initial response, which is fair enough, but he did end up offering a precis of his thesis: 'I just saw so many parallels with the intentions, communities, identities and relationship dynamics of fandom spaces that it stopped being a cute observation. When I started digging more, it became apparent that fans had always existed in politics and so had obsessive anti-fans, but the bits that make it fandom rather than individual fans or grouped as a fanbase were a bit newer.

'The three things that make a fandom are your interest in a cultural property being part of your identity, you joining a community and that being intentional. Anti-fandom is the same thing but in opposition to a cultural property.

'As soon as it moves from a private interest to something you want to engage with other people about, then you're in a fandom. Anyone who watches PMQs and thinks it is important and discusses it with other people is doing the same thing as someone watching the football or cricket or listening to TalkSport.'

I like this theory a lot, both because it is very astute and because it puts my own experience into context. Perhaps it is not that embarrassing that I got into political journalism because I liked the memes; and if it is, at least I'm not the only one. More broadly, Andrews' point on the link between politics and identity strikes me as the crux of the issue.

As discussed in this very book ad nauseam, living online does odd things to your sense of self; it should not be surprising that politics ended up becoming such a magnet to people spending too much time on the internet. At the risk of repeating myself, things also changed – not for the better – when everyone joined us online. Suddenly, people who did not have a handle on how to behave online started spending hours and days in Facebook groups and on Twitter. Malevolent and cynical forces realised they had suddenly gained a few million eyeballs they previously couldn't reach quite as directly, and they gave their shiny new audiences what they wanted. There was money to be earned and power to be gained in exploiting the relative gullibility of people faced with a medium they hadn't grown up with, with predictable results. Fake and sexed-up news went viral because of formerly offline boomers who assumed that something being published on a website meant it had to be true, and everything got worse. Those very people became radicalised – on Brexit, Trump, or anything else you can think of – without meaning to. They just got sucked into our vortex, without the means to realise what was happening to them.

It is not something I really want to explore in depth, both because it has been reported on extensively by everyone else already and because they are not the people I set out to write about. If you would like to read about grandmothers falling for QAnon or divorced dads becoming white supremacists, most media outlets have you covered. Instead, I would like to return to some themes closer to home. More specifically, I want to talk about the extent to which I no longer want to talk about politics.

It is a very sad state of affairs; most of the friendships I have today started online because of our mutual interest in politics and the news, and I worked very hard in order to make politics and the news my everyday job. Now I am worried I want out.

I am exhausted, and have been for a long time. As a young progressive who grew up online, I have been expected to care about everything for so very long. I had to read about earthquakes in Asia and famines in South America; the plight of a group of trans youths in Alabama and the tragic death of a girl in Kenya. Every day there is a new thing – no! one million new things! – and I have to care about all of them.

I have to donate money and sign a petition and write to my MP and use a hashtag and post a picture and read a thread and boycott a brand and retweet a post so that all my friends see it. No one has ever explored the possibility that I could not care about some of these things; it is assumed that I do care, about all of them.

Every day I wake up and one million terrible things have happened in the world, because the world is a very big place and we are not good people. Ignorance was once bliss but now neutrality in situations of injustice means choosing the side of the oppressor. Nothing is ever good because there is always something going wrong. If even one person drowns, all of our lungs are filling up with water.

It is overwhelming and I worry it has made me a meaner and smaller person. At some point, heaven knows when, I decided I could not care about all these things anymore and so now I care about very little. There is a story in the news at time of writing about an alpaca with tuberculosis and I really hope the alpaca gets killed soon so we can stop hearing about it. Donald Trump was president for four years and for several of those years I, like many others, just refused to read news about the US.

I was well-meaning once, then I had enough; I cannot carry all the miseries of the world on my shoulders. No one can. We were not built to have constant access to a screen on which thousands of people can beg for our attention every minute of every day. Normal, everyday humans should not have to behave like ambassadors, posting solemn messages of sadness and solidarity whenever something tragic happens.

The bitter icing on the cake is that there is no one for me to be angry at. Of course, if you know of a great injustice happening on your doorstep you will want as many people as possible to know about it, in the hope that it will help get it resolved. Global outrage can do wonderful and powerful things, why wouldn't you try to make the world care about the plights of those close to your heart? And if people who see themselves as caring and progressive do not have it in them to hit a button or add their name to a petition, do they really deserve the fuzzy feeling that comes from thinking you are a good person? As far as I can tell, the only solutions are to either care about everything endlessly until you are entirely burnt out, or to decide that you are not that good a person after all. Neither is especially comfortable, which is a shame because being a reactionary online sounds like a lot of fun. If the internet managed to bring marginalised people together, making them more influential and louder in the process, it did much the same thing to some of the worst people alive.

Because social media has more or less put an end to gatekeeping in political discourse, it also became possible for bigots of all stripes to meet some kindred spirits, emboldening their stances in the process. If you were a lone sexist crank living alone in a small town, there was not much you could do about your beliefs. You knew you were in a small minority and that your views were not generally accepted by mainstream society.

Once you were handed a keyboard and an internet connection, things changed. Suddenly there were dozens and hundreds of sexist cranks you could talk to; you could become part of a group, make some friends, and discuss all those beliefs that you'd had to keep to yourself all this time. Hell, you could even go and be sexist online together! The dream! I'm being a bit glib here, of course, but this is basically what has been happening online for some time now. Io Dodds has reported on the phenomenon before and told me this: 'I was talking to an academic called Kishonna Gray for an investigation I did into far right radicalisation in video game communities. She has studied the far right and alt right video game communities and said that there's still this narrative that they're isolated and lonely when in fact, they have an amazing community together, but their focus is still so much on that rejection or what happened to them. I think it's really important we recognise how these people have found each other in these communities, and that creates the confirmation bias and their racism feeds each other and that's part of how they get radicalised.

'Part of how they get radicalised is that these are pleasant communities for these people, especially because they've been driven out of other communities for being racist, right? This reminds me of that thing about Wario and Waluigi, that they're just these two nice evil guys who found each other.'

Then there's the small matter of identity; in the real

world you could be a bit of a loner who happened to be quite racist, but if suddenly you managed to make all these friends online because of your racism, that racism will end up becoming one of your defining traits.

As Io pointed out, it is what often gets missed when trying to understand radicalisation online; it is nice to have friends and to feel like you belong. The problem for the rest of us, of course, is that these racists – or misogynists, or transphobes, or a combination of all of the above – thrive on making everyone else's lives worse. I should know, I am a woman who dares to be online.

I have received death threats and rape threats; dozens of men have left insulting and horrible comments underneath pictures of myself I posted online. My inboxes have been flooded with abuse and, on two occasions, my profiles on dating apps were leaked and tweeted out, with people encouraged to mock me for them.

It's an odd thing to talk about because it sounds very dramatic written down but really, I don't hugely care anymore. It stung at first, because of course it did, but I do believe that human beings can get used to more or less anything if given enough time, and eventually, I got used to it. There is nothing I can do about it, after all – I may as well let it wash over me, because it's the only way I can win.

I know that my life is better than all of theirs and if

sending me abuse can make them that little bit better, who am I to object? These are clearly not very happy people and it is nice that they have found a hobby.

It is possible that I'm being patronising as a defence mechanism and I believe I was for quite a long time, but it has become pretty sincere now; I cannot bring myself to care anymore. Could social media companies do more so that the women growing up today have it better than us? Of course. Will they? I'm not holding my breath. In the meantime, this is what we are left with: a political arena that brought people in from far and wide by educating them and opening their minds, then left them to fend for themselves. I'm grateful that I fell down this particular rabbit hole – I wouldn't be writing this today if I hadn't. I also wouldn't have got to read the thoughts and opinions of so many people around the world; people from so many different backgrounds and with so many different experiences. There is so much I know and have thought about, and it has changed my life for the better. Still, this doesn't change the fact that I'm now yearning to retreat from the political side of the internet. I wonder how many others feel the same; anecdotally, I know of countless people who have stepped back from Twitter for good.

The world was always overwhelming but we didn't have to always know about it; we made our lives bigger then realised there was value in relative ignorance. I cannot change how much strife and suffering there is in the world but I can change how much I know about it. I can also decide not to make my life a never-ending series of debates conducted in bad faith – there are better things I can be doing with my finite time on this earth.

My worry, however, is that the people staying and enjoying themselves are the ones who made the political internet inhabitable in the first place. Should we stay and fight? I'm sure some people will, but I no longer see it as my duty. Why should it be? I came here for the memes and the beautiful men, no one told me I was enlisting in a war. There is little honour in surrendering, but I have made my peace with it: having a quiet life is reward enough.

Stay Weird

As you know, I had a music website when I was a teen-ager, which was written in French and, by the standards of the day, was reasonably successful. As you probably do not remember, because I only mentioned it in passing, I have always been interested in fashion and spent my teenage years longing to get into Fashion Week. This yearning intensified when I moved to London, and it all came to a head one morning in January 2011.

I was 19 and lying in bed, very hungover. I was thinking about the fact that I hadn't been on holiday since moving in September 2009, and that I couldn't afford to go abroad. This made me think about the concept of holidays. What makes a good holiday? A good holiday, I decided, meant going to places you had not been to before, doing things you did not do in your day-to-day life and meeting new and interesting people.

Suddenly, I got an idea. I could not afford to go abroad because I was a student, but I could try to do something in London that would tick all those boxes: I could try to get into Fashion Week. My plan was simple and low-effort, because I was certain it would not work and I had a very bad headache.

I went to edit my music website and added a tab at the top, called 'fashion'. I went to edit that tab so that, when you clicked on it, it said: 'this page is currently under maintenance! please check again later!' Once that was done, I applied for a press pass for London Fashion Week, explaining that I was the editor of a music *and fashion* website.

To my genuine surprise, I received an email a few days later, informing me that I had been accepted. It was hilarious and unexpected but only the first step; the real test was to then apply to get tickets to all the individual fashion shows. I spent an afternoon firing off emails to every single designer on the spreadsheet, explaining I was an accredited French fashion journalist covering Fashion Week in London, and waited.

Over the course of about ten days, I ended up receiving around 25 paper invitations to shows in the post; as it turns out, the fashion world is very – for lack of a better word – old-fashioned. I was thrilled and bewildered; the whole thing had been a con and I'd got away with it.

When Fashion Week started, I went to all the shows I'd received tickets for; I was out of the house from 9am to about 2am for five consecutive days, running from catwalks to parties then back again. It was exhilarating and occasionally character building. As I found out the hard way, for example, Fashion Week 'breakfasts' often only include champagne and Bloody Marys. If you make the mistake of arriving there with an empty stomach, it is likely that you will find yourself too drunk to walk down the Strand at 10:45am. If this happens to you and you decide to carry on drinking, you will probably be so sloshed by 1am that you will end up doing some things that will see you barred from a private members' club.

In short: I was 19 years old and I had a tremendous time. I did not write a word about it, of course; as I found out, there is a difference between enjoying fashion and being able to write interestingly about it. I knew that this meant my con had to come to an end, but I had no regrets. I'd wanted a holiday and got to have one without ever needing to pack up and leave.

Still, in August that year, I decided to try my luck again. I put the fake 'fashion' tab back in its place and sent my accreditation request. I was convinced it wouldn't work; surely, someone had noticed that I had attended a full season without publishing a single piece on it? My application was accepted nearly immediately and I burst out laughing.

I spent a day sending requests to designers again and off we went. In the end, I attended many seasons of London Fashion Week; on my fourth or fifth, I was upgraded to VIP Media, meaning I could get into any show without a ticket and did not have to queue for any of them. I should add that I had stopped updating the music website entirely by 2012. It wasn't even that I'd faked writing about fashion; by the last few seasons, I wasn't using that blog at all. Still, the invites kept arriving.

Well, they did until 2013, when the press office – not unreasonably – asked to see some proof that my blog had any readers at all. I knew I could not provide any, as my blog no longer had any readers, so I left it at that. It wasn't sad; I had reached the point when Fashion Week (absurdly) felt like work, which defeated the entire point. I was only ever going because I wanted a distraction and once it became a normal part of my life, it lost its charm entirely.

The year 2013 was also a very different time from 2010, in the fashion industry and elsewhere. I'd managed to slip through the net in the beginning because serious people with serious jobs did not quite know what to do with us yet. They were aware that there were young people online with influence and fans but they could not quite tell the difference between the bona fide celebrities and the charming layabouts. The Tavi Gevinsons of this world had convinced them that they needed to engage with the teenage bloggers but they did not really know what to do with those kids. On our side, the internet still felt like a silly and weird playground where nothing was really real, and so we mostly tried to have fun with it.

I was not thinking about money or my future career when I was running my blog and doing things I shouldn't have been doing; for the most part, I was trying to have a good time. The internet of the 2000s did not really feel like it could lead to serious, professional success. Instead, it was used to bypass the serious, professional ways in which people made their careers, like mischievous DIY.

I talked about this with Blaine Harrison, who plays in the Mystery Jets. I first met him in 2008 when his band played in my hometown and I interviewed them; we all went out drinking after the gig and he asked me for a cigarette because he'd quit smoking but regretted it. I gave him one and we talked for a while; to my horror, I read his MySpace tour blog a few days later and found out that the cigarette had made him throw up in the tour bus.

About ten years later, I saw him in a pub in Peckham;

I went to apologise for the cigarette incident, convinced he'd forgotten about it, but he remembered it well. We talked for a while and have remained vaguely in touch since. I emailed him because I wanted to know more about his formative musical years.

'We started the band while we were still in school. We sent our demos to every label in London and would play all these shitty club nights in the hopes that some non-existent A+R scout would show up to sign a bunch of scruffy 17-year-olds and their dad, but they never did. In the end, we just got sick of all our friends being charged £7 or £8 at the door, which was a lot in 2003 money, so we decided to put on our own parties and let the industry come to us.

'My dad runs a boatyard on Eel Pie Island, on the Thames in Twickenham, and there used to be a famous blues club there which everyone from The Stones to Hendrix to Pink Floyd played at, back in the day. It burned down in the seventies, so we thought we'd bring some of that spirit back to the birthplace of British Blues and that's when things really began for us.

'Myself and our guitarist William were at art school nearby so would print out our own handmade flyers, pin them on the message boards and post a group message out on MySpace (often spam other bands' message boards too), usually a day or two before, telling everyone to bring their own booze and everyone they knew. We'd book anywhere between five to 10 other bands a night, playing 20-minute sets, and didn't charge anything at the door. No sound checks, no backstage and no security. It was complete chaos.

'We'd put on a party every couple of months and over a period of about a year and a half, they went from 20 people sitting cross-legged on the floor to people showing up in their hundreds. We'd have people falling in the river, swinging from the light fittings, smoking cigarettes indoors, and the room was covered floor-to-ceiling in Moroccan carpets so it was a huge fire hazard. On two occasions, people left in ambulances.

'The last party was kind of legendary. Seven hundred people showed up and half the people that squeezed into the room were music industry scouts, managers, and booking agents, who ended up signing most of the bands on the bill. And then the noise police showed up and served us a £20,000 noise abatement order if we tried to do it again. So it ended there, but that was the right time to kill it.'

Being able to use their own place to host gigs changed everything, of course, but the internet also had its part to play. More than any other website, MySpace turned out to be a game changer for the Mystery Jets and others, a way to build a scene without relying on record labels or established venues.

'For bands, it created a whole new way of mobilising your fan base and being able to be much more spontaneous with everything. We take it for granted now, but the ability to just drop a new track or announce a show at the very last minute – that hadn't really been possible in the same way before Myspace.

'You suddenly didn't need to pay for fly posters or ad campaigns in magazines anymore, because word just got around so quickly. We would often put demos of our new tracks up online for a couple of weeks and then take them down. People would rip them and share them around, and it meant that by the time of your next show everyone already knew all the lyrics.'

As one of the fans who downloaded, shared and obsessively listened to those MySpace demos, I can confirm that these times were glorious. If I'm being honest, they were also unbearable; I spent so much time listening to increasingly obscure unsigned bands that the idea of buying an album from a major label artist felt absurd.

Hours and days were lost trawling from MySpace

band to MySpace band, desperately trying to find the next big thing before anyone else. I was hardly reinventing the wheel, of course – indie snobbery has existed for as long as electric guitars have. Still, this feeling of being able to do whatever we wanted and being linked to all these other kids doing whatever they wanted felt thrilling. The bands were DIY, the bloggers writing about them were DIY, and so too were the photographers, party promoters and everyone else.

No one was trying to get rich or go big; if anything, the people looking like they were after mainstream success were usually shunned. Big corporations were seen as boring and bland and the antithesis of what we collectively stood for. We didn't have to go work for them and soften our edges, we could just be ourselves and do our own thing.

This particular scene didn't last, but then I don't believe it was ever going to. Indie music was quite edgy then it became cool then it became mainstream then it stopped being cool. That is the life cycle of a music genre and anyway, one cannot cling on to the music of their teenage years forever more.

I'm fine with that; instead, what makes me sad is that this entire way of behaving and thinking didn't last either. For a start, there is nowhere for young and upcoming artists to slowly build a profile and release their unpolished, half-finished demos anymore.

MySpace is gone and Spotify will always favour music with the backing of large labels. Instagram, meanwhile, can only ever be gamed by people who look nice on top of sounding good – it isn't the same.

Not that the online infrastructure is the worst of our problems; the culture has irreversibly changed as well. It is now possible to obtain global, overwhelming and near-instant success from the internet and that has broken everything. Videos are monetised and brands sponsor everything and everyone; if you are doing something online, it is assumed that you are trying to make some money from it.

The change in mindset has been absolute; far from being a stupid playground away from the grown-ups, the internet is now the place to be if you want to preen in front of people promisingly waving piles of cash. To be a bit kinder, it is also where a lot of us work now: how could it have remained a DIY wonderland?

I discussed this with journalist Tom Phillips and he saw what I meant; together, we tried to identify the point when everything changed. This is what he told me: 'I wouldn't identify it as a specific moment but there was a tipping point, where a company fucks up on social media and everybody makes the joke about how the intern's getting fired, and people started going, "I'm sorry, we are now a decade into 'social media manager' being a highly skilled job – couldn't we stop 'the intern runs the Twitter account' jokes?" There was that realisation that even if we were doing these things for fun, even if a bunch of early adopters had lucked into jobs, suddenly this thing that was fun was our job.

'It was an economy. It was an industry. It was something that you could be good and bad at, and that you could get better at. You can't avoid being an industry. When you're in industry, that is a tide you cannot turn back. You can't maintain a space of just fun and creativity by denying that you're part of an economy. Fun, creative spaces will not maintain themselves on their own because they will evolve and they will break down, especially when these are in fact people's livelihoods. There is a responsibility that comes with that.'

As someone who was once hired in newsrooms as 'the token young person who understands the internet', I cannot disagree with his theory. Money and people arrived and suddenly nothing could be fun in the same way anymore. We transitioned from our teenage years into adulthood and the internet did the same; as it turns out, it is tough to be carefree if you suddenly have money and responsibilities.

Still, I'm not sure the culture change had to be this thorough. I have spent a lot of the past six, seven, eight years gawping at influencers and feeling like an ape, left behind by evolution. Why are they all so bland? How can someone become famous for wearing clothes that they have been given for free? Why would you be young and carefree and determined to willingly associate yourself with large and faceless corporations?

Why would you follow someone who never says or does anything daring or interesting? Why would you celebrate someone being paid by a brand to advertise their products to you? Why would you spend so much time looking at digitally retouched pictures of women who already were traditionally beautiful but now look otherworldly, all so they can advertise some more products to you? Why, why, why?

Whenever I think about this, I end up thinking about a piece Taylor Lorenz wrote for the *Atlantic* in 2018 and which made me feel nauseous. It was about young women pretending to be influencers, by buying products themselves but tagging the brands in the Instagram posts and writing the captions to make it seem like they had been given everything for free. Just look at this:

'When Allie, a 15-year-old lifestyle influencer who asked to be referred to by a pseudonym, scrolls through her Instagram feed, sometimes the whole thing seems like an ad. There's a fellow teen beauty influencer bragging about her sponsorship with Maybelline, a high-school sophomore she knows touting his brand campaign with Voss water. None of these promotions, however, is real. Allie is friends with the people posting, so she knows. She once faked a water sponsorship herself. "People pretend to have brand deals to seem cool," Allie said.'

People pretend to have brand deals to seem cool! I have never felt more like an ape gawping at a screen. People pretend to have brand deals to seem cool. The internet was a terrible idea and I'm heartbroken.

I realise I'm sounding very dramatic but I can't help it; I know my generation's disgust at the idea that anyone may wish to one day make a living out of what they love was ridiculous, but it is all I have. Well, I'm not even sure it is a generational phenomenon; there are many people my age who are making a lot of money on the internet by being very bland. I once spoke to a woman a few years older than me who had done some promoted posts about ham on her Instagram. She was very happy about it. I had to smile and nod at someone telling me about ham.

Still, the odd thing about all this is that the internet still loves grifters and people who manipulate others for fun. Caroline Calloway is one of them; she is exactly my age and I cannot help but be in awe of how annoying she is.

She joined Instagram in 2012 and became famous for being blonde and white and posting long captions underneath her posts. In 2016 she got a book deal and announced in 2017 that the book would not be happening after all. In 2018 she was still famous and advertised some creative workshops on how to become famous like her, but those failed to materialise as well.

In 2019, her best friend Natalie Beach published an essay explaining that 'Caroline Calloway' was a con and that she herself had written many of the long Instagram captions Calloway had become famous for. That should have been the end of it but it wasn't; a month before the essay was published, Caroline Calloway had hosted a workshop called 'the Scam'. She knew exactly what she was, she was not trying to hide it.

In 2020 she announced that she was going to publish a memoir called *Scammer*. She never wrote the book. I was asked to interview Calloway that year and turned it down, because I realised that there was no scenario in which I could come out of that exchange victorious. There probably was not a scenario in which the ending was neutral either; whatever happens to Caroline Calloway has to be a triumph for her and an embarrassment to whoever she is facing.

I both loathe her and am oddly attached to her; there is something off-putting and off-kilter about her that is incredibly compelling. She keeps nearly reaching bona fide fame then shooting herself in the foot by doing something distasteful. Last time I checked, she was selling a skincare product she had made herself, called Snake Oil.

Caroline Calloway feels like a perverted parody of these influencers who ruin everything with their fake and beige authenticity. I have no idea who she actually is or what she actually wants, which is oddly refreshing. I also like that people can't take their eyes away from her; it shows that the internet cannot be entirely taken over by people who will twist themselves into whatever shape in order to be traditionally successful. Still, her controversial and bizarre fame could only have come about in the internet of the late 2010s. What would have been the point of Calloway in 2009? So many of us were sort of grifters back then and culture was too fragmented for anyone to become famous – or infamous – across the board.

There was no real money to be made quite yet, so instead we exploited any loophole we could find to make our lives a bit more fun. I suppose this should be the point at which I confess that, perhaps, I am overindulging in nostalgia and my people did not have it entirely right. After all, many of the people I interviewed here ended up getting jobs that largely involve sitting in front of a computer and being broadly good at the internet. I would not be where I am if it hadn't been for that cultural shift either; 2009 Marie had a tremendous time, but 2021 Marie has a very decent income.

Sometimes you just can't have your cake and eat it.

For a while I was even paid to be fun and weird on the internet, for an organisation I will not bother naming. I got to my desk in the morning and my job was to write purposefully silly things that would entertain people who were loitering online because they were bored. I got to pay my rent by doing this for just under a year.

I could have paid my rent this way for longer but I left after ten months because I could feel my soul getting destroyed, bit by bit. I spent my days writing pointless things because a media organisation wanted to make money by aping the pointless things people wrote online when they were bored.

The editors and execs of the mid-2010s did not really understand the internet and thought they could win by replicating what they were already seeing. It worked until it didn't; it was fun until it wasn't. I left because it became a bone-crushingly depressing job and I stopped reading quirky, silly and relatable things online a few years after that because it soon became clear that most people writing them were also bone-crushingly depressed. There was little joy left; no genuine enthusiasm or authenticity.

Every time something exciting or novel happened there would be a journalist or social media person there to make a professional version of it and they would suck all the fun out of it. *BuzzFeed* had hired an army of online people in their early twenties because they were the best at spotting new trends and stories likely to go viral. You could stumble upon an amusing page and blink; in seconds, *BuzzFeed* had covered it to death.

I worked at *BuzzFeed* for a year, I should know. Does this mean that I'm one of those sell-outs I spent a portion of this essay decrying? Am I no better than an influencer posing with some ham? I want to believe, in my heart of hearts, that I'm better than an influencer posing with some ham. Am I?

Maybe we're the same because neither of us is the problem. I fell into online content because it felt like the easiest way into journalism in the early 2010s and I'm a naturally lazy woman. People my age and younger pretend that brands are paying them to do their advertisement because, I assume, it feels easier than having a real job – I can't fault them for that, even if I really want to.

I do judge the people who, for whatever reason, have come to enjoy having their social media timelines turned into streams of shameless product placements, but they should be allowed to be dull. Being boring is not a crime. What is heart-wrenching, on the other hand, is that the very structure of the current internet means that the people who want to be more interesting than that no longer have obvious ways in which to do so. Because the internet now allows people to dream big, it has become harder to dream small and only aim to cause some low-level mischief.

I never would have wanted to have as much of a profile as Caroline Calloway; all I cared about was drinking free champagne ten days a year and pretending to work in fashion. All the Mystery Jets wanted was to play music for their friends without relying on the whims of the music industry. All we wanted was to do our own thing and have a good time.

I can't say I'm not glad I got a career instead, and I'm sure Blaine Harrison is pleased his band eventually got signed to a major label. I just wish we could have kept our wonderland, if not for us then at least for today's nerdy and naughty kids. Where else can so much trouble be caused with so few consequences?

4

WHERE ARE WE GOING?

Kids Like You and Me

I began this book by saying that I didn't really want to write it; it wasn't really true and largely a rhetorical trick to introduce one of the themes I wanted to discuss in the introduction. It was a bit of a lie, but it was harmless.

As it turned out, I did not really enjoy writing this book. I am not one of those writers who usually hates writing; those people are incredibly annoying. No, I like writing; it is absurd that I get to do it for a living. Sometimes I wonder if it should even be allowed. Still, this was not a pleasant experience; for the most part, it made me sad, anxious or both. The former probably shouldn't have been a surprise; after all, I was attempting to chronicle the slow death of a world I loved. Forcing myself to confront this reality was never going to be very entertaining. The latter was a more complex beast; as it turns out, the internet is good at tricking you into believing that every experience you have on it is both entirely unique and entirely universal. As a result, every story and anecdote instantly became agonising.

Did you read this and nod in recognition throughout? Did my experiences mirror yours, even if they were not quite the same? Do you feel a bit less alone now, knowing that there is someone out there who went through the same things you did? Or were you alienated by it all and are you coming out of it disappointed that it missed the mark?

I know you cannot answer any of these questions to me directly and it kills me. I got online when I was young because I was lonely and I wrote this book about that decision because I carry a lot of love in my heart for the people who did the same as me. What's the point of all this if I did not manage to give our people a voice and put some of our lives into words? It all sounds terribly grand, of course, but sometimes that is fine – we cannot all be humble all of the time.

✳ ✳ ✳

I keep trying to avoid writing this by opening new tabs instead but there is nothing for me to do in those tabs. I have been refreshing my Twitter timeline so frequently that there is nothing there for me to read. Instagram announced to me this morning that I had seen all the posts available to me and, since then, the people I follow have had the temerity not to post any new ones.

I went on Facebook then immediately remembered that there is nothing for me on Facebook anymore, so I clicked on my 'memories' tab. On this day in 2015, I was begging friends for last-minute accommodation in Bournemouth because I was unexpectedly going to the Liberal Democrats' Party Conference.

On this day in 2011, I was 'close to the Royal Opera House' and asked my friends for company – 'you'll be rewarded with lots of champagne' – because I was at London Fashion Week and between shows.

On this day in 2009, I announced that I was off to Leeds for the weekend, to visit a French friend I had met through my blog in 2006 because we both liked the Horrors. I remember that weekend well because I was 17 and I tried to sleep with a man who was 24 and he refused, and I was very offended. Wherever you are today, Martin, I hope you're having a nice life. More men in their twenties should refuse to sleep with women they know to be 17.

I ran out of Facebook memories to look at so I looked at WhatsApp instead and there was nothing of interest there either. Well, there were many messages I have needed to reply to for many days, but if it hasn't happened yet, will it ever happen? Probably not.

I went back to Twitter and there were a few new tweets to read and that kept me busy for three or four minutes. Do you know how aware I am of the irony of it all, of the fact that I am desperately trying to be entertained by a dull and lifeless internet because I am trying to avoid writing about how dull and lifeless the internet has become?

I could not be more aware of it.

✵ ✵ ✵

I was having a drink with a friend who is my age the other day and we realised we sounded old. She had been to a dinner with some people in their very early twenties the week before and was telling me about it. We sat there, drinking margaritas that cost £9 each because we are no longer 20 years old, and we scratched our heads.

The two young women were not unlike us – creative, a bit odd, ambitious but keen to do their own thing – and they spoke in a way we did not recognise. They were obsessed with 'the hustle' and convinced that by the time they reached our age, they would be obscenely rich and successful, all thanks to the internet.

It was, my friend reported, never quite clear what

would bring them said wealth or fame; they just assumed that by being online enough, they would eventually find a way to earn piles of cash. Would it be fashion, an app, a start-up, generic influencing? Perhaps one of them; perhaps several; perhaps something else entirely. Something was bound to come up eventually.

It was a puzzling and sad conversation because we were both struck by the fact that people a decade younger than us had grown up in an internet we did not recognise at all. There was this chasm between us and we had no idea how to breach it – their formative years had simply been too different from ours.

They were born around the year 2000 and there was never a point in their life during which the internet did not exist. By the time they got their own laptops and smartphones, the internet was already fully formed.

There is no doubt about it: the internet now belongs to them and I have no idea what they do on it. I assume that TikTok is at least a part of their online existence, but I don't have it on my phone so I'm not sure. They still use Instagram stories, I'm told, but I don't know about much else.

More importantly, I don't understand the texture of their online lives; the types of conversations that they have and exactly who they decide to have those conversations with. I don't know if they feel like they are the same people online that they are in real life. I would ask them but if you are 20 years old and you have never known anything else, you are probably not self-aware enough to come up with a satisfactory answer.

I'm also not sure I want to know; one of the reasons why I never downloaded TikTok is that it annoyed me when grown-ups invaded my internet and I don't want to do the same thing to newer generations. I know there are a lot of grown-ups on TikTok and that this particular fight is lost, but I didn't want anything to do with it. It is, after all, my belief that the internet is at its best when every group or generation is allowed to have its own spaces. Staying away from this one felt like the polite thing to do, even if it was essentially pointless.

I do not want to ruin new platforms by joining them but I increasingly have less and less interest in the platforms I have been on for years. I only really use Twitter and Instagram these days and I do not feel especially enthusiastic about either of them. Where am I to go?

I discovered a great bar and told everyone about it and now it is dreadful, but I still cannot get myself to leave it. I grew up in it and some of the best and worst moments of my life happened here – I may as well grab a stool and sit stonily in the corner.

It annoys me that I cannot end this by announcing

that I'm leaving the internet. It would have been a neat arc: I escaped from real life by coming here and now I'm escaping again from whatever this has become. Sadly, the truth is: I do not want to leave the internet. My entire job and most of my life are on there – on here – and I have no interest in only ever living in the real world. I wouldn't even know how to go about it. What do people do with their fingers when they're not typing? What do they look at when there isn't a screen nearby? This is why I'm sad that soon I will no longer be writing this book. I know that I said at the start of this essay that writing it made me sad, but that doesn't mean that finishing it will not make me sad as well – I am a woman online, I am exceptionally good at being sad. Finishing this and moving on to other work will mean propelling myself back into the current day, which is not something I am looking forward to. I am already nostalgic about the time I got to spend steeped in nostalgia.

I cannot help who I am; when I left primary school at the age of nine, I distinctly remember turning around one last time, alone, thinking, 'a page is turning' and shedding a tear. I was a very dramatic child and am a marginally less dramatic adult. Living a real life in the present just isn't my favourite way of going about things – a little delusion is always nice. I suppose this is the lesson I have learned in the past few months; the conclusion I had to bring myself to. I'm having a hard time letting go of the internet of my youth because it allowed me to think of real life as a little bit less real.

To this day, I tweet about every bad thing that happens to me because once you tell a story to someone, the burden is no longer entirely yours. If I have to think about a way to write entertainingly about an unpleasant incident in under 280 characters, I'm no longer the person who suffered the unpleasant incident. Instead, I am a storyteller; Fleabag looking at the camera from the corner of her eye.

If I have to deal with my electricity bills and the fact that I cannot quite afford them then I may as well joke about it online, turning it into a performance in the process. Real life doesn't need to be entirely real all of the time. I'm sure some people will argue that that is a bad thing and that a woman who is about to turn 30 should simply make her peace with adult life being, for the most part, quite tedious. There is only so much reminiscing I can do before I realise that I really do just need to get a pension.

Maybe this will happen; there is a world in which this book comes out and, by the time you sit down to read it, I will have stopped looking at screens all day long and started living in the real world. I doubt this will be the case. Instead, I like to think that I will have found some new niches and crevasses online, and that I will happily be hiding in them by then.

In fact, I wonder if this has already started happening. I mentioned earlier that I now have a locked Twitter account, which I created in 2020. It was borne out of urgent necessity as I suddenly felt I could no longer handle the amount of abuse I received on my public account, but it feels, in retrospect, like the beginning of something.

Everything I did on the internet for 15 years made my life a little bit bigger and more open. Life on MSN Messenger was small and life as a blogger was wider; it got wider still with MySpace and Facebook, then eventually with Twitter. There were more people I talked to and more people I could talk to if I wanted to; each new space contained more possibilities than the one before that.

In this context, the creation of my private account was oddly seismic, as it represented the reversal of a trend that had been unfolding for the majority of my existence. It is striking because I do not believe it is a move that happened in a vacuum. More and more, I find myself clicking on Twitter and Instagram profiles and realising that they are private. We spread and spread and spread and now, exhausted and weary, we are retreating.

I wonder how conscious those decisions are; I did not realise what I was doing or aiming for until I was able to look at it in hindsight.

I don't know the extent to which people realise that what they miss is the old internet, the places that felt human-sized and the communities that could shape them for years on end. A part of me believes that they will come back one day and that they may not be entirely the same, but they will feel safe and fun again.

The latter is the most important part: I want my internet to be fun. If you picked up this book out of curiosity, this is what I would like you to understand: we just had so much fun in those years, it was brilliant.

The internet was our collective Plan B because, for whatever reason, we couldn't fit in with real people – but what a Plan B it was. If I could do it all over again, I would choose to get mocked and bullied again, just so I could seek solace inside that screen. It was perfect.

And maybe this is where we have to end it. We escaped because we had no other choice and it wasn't always painless but really, it was perfect. No one before our time will ever really understand us and neither will anyone born after us; it was our world and we milked it for all it was worth.

Parts of that universe are still everywhere online, if you know where to look. The internet built us and, for a little while, we built it in return. It collapsed because it was always going to; we were idiot children and we had no idea what we were doing. Everyone joined us and everything was ruined. Maybe it doesn't matter; a part of me will always live in those spaces and a part of my heart will always belong to the old internet. It is all we can ask for in the end, isn't it? To have had a tremendous time and come out the other side weirder and happier. It's all we can ask for.

ACKNOWLEDGEMENTS

Thanks to David K for giving me the title of the book; to Agnes F for your reassuring presence; to Madiya A, Imogen P and everyone at Bonnier for making it all happen; to the people who agreed to be interviewed for this book for your brilliant insights; to everyone I met online over the past 15 years for changing my life.